We thought this
may come in handy
when you start entertaining
with all that fine + casual
china! Feel free to experiment
on us if you like

Merry Christmas

Love, Phil + Susie

Casual Occasions
Cookbook

CASUAL OCCASIONS
COOKBOOK

GENERAL EDITOR

CHUCK WILLIAMS

MENU CONCEPTS & RECIPES

JOYCE GOLDSTEIN

PHOTOGRAPHY

ALLAN ROSENBERG & ALLEN V. LOTT

WELDON OWEN

First published in the U.S.A. in 1995 by
Weldon Owen Inc.
814 Montgomery Street
San Francisco, CA 94133

In collaboration with
Williams–Sonoma
100 North Point
San Francisco, CA 94133

The Williams-Sonoma Entertaining Series
conceived and produced by Weldon Owen Inc.

WILLIAMS-SONOMA
Founder/Vice-Chairman: Chuck Williams

WELDON OWEN INC.
President: John Owen
Publisher: Wendely Harvey
Managing Editor: Tori Ritchie
Project Coordinator: Genevieve Morgan
Consulting Editor: Norman Kolpas
Copy Editor: Sharon Silva
Editorial Assistant: Claire Sanchez
Art Director: John Bull
Designer: Nancy Campana
Production: Stephanie Sherman, Tarji Mickelson,
  Jim Obata
Photography: Allan Rosenberg and Allen V. Lott
Locations and Primary Prop Stylist: Sandra Griswold
Assistant Prop Stylist: Elizabeth Ruegg
Consulting Stylist: Karen Nicks
Food Stylist: Heidi Gintner
Assistant Food Stylist: Danielle Di Salvo
Wine Consultant: Evan Goldstein
Menu Illustrations: Diana Reiss-Koncar
Appendix Illustrations: Alice Harth

Library of Congress Cataloging-in-Publication Data:

Casual occasions cookbook/general editor Chuck
  Williams, menu concepts & recipes Joyce Goldstein,
  photography Allan Rosenberg & Allen V. Lott.
        p.   cm. — (Williams-Sonoma entertaining series)
     Includes index.
     ISBN 1-875137-18-1
     1. Cookery 2. Entertaining 3. Menus.
     I. Williams, Chuck. II. Title. III. Series.
  TX731.G567 1995
  642'.4--dc20   94-18474
                                          CIP
Produced in Hong Kong by Mandarin Offset.
Printed in Hong Kong

A Weldon Owen Production

A Note on Weights and Measures:
*All recipes include customary U.S., U.K. and metric
measurements. Conversions are based on a standard
developed for these books and have been rounded off.
Actual weights may vary.*

Front Cover: Family Birthday Party, see page 115.

CONTENTS

INTRODUCTION

CASUAL DINNERS

Casual Parties

Entertaining Basics

*I*NTRODUCTION

ANY GATHERING, REGARDLESS of the season, event or size of guest list can be a casual occasion. Wherever you live and whatever your means, this book will help you welcome friends and family to your home with an air of informality that allows everyone involved to relax, from the moment the occasion is planned and the invitations are issued until the last person leaves and the final dish has been stacked in the cupboard.

From start to finish, the pages ahead are geared toward making your casual entertaining easier and more enjoyable, whether you're giving a party to mark a birthday or anniversary or just inviting a few people over for Sunday night supper. In the menus and recipes, as in the many ideas for planning and hosting a party, the philosophy that prevails is that—with just a little effort— any event, no matter how understated or casual, can be truly stylish and memorable.

Chuck Williams   *Joyce Goldstein*

Entertaining with Ease

As the fifteen menus in this book vividly demonstrate, the word *casual* can take on many different meanings, from a backyard barbecue to a kitchen breakfast to an engagement party. What all of these occasions have in common is easy hospitality and the underlying principle that pleasure comes whenever good food is generously shared. Even though casual meals may be far more relaxed than formal parties, they still call for some thought and planning.

Choosing the Menu

The menus in the *Casual Occasions Cookbook* have been created and planned by master chef and cookbook author Joyce Goldstein. To help guide you in your selection of a menu, the section called "Casual Dinners" focuses on evening gatherings of two to eight people; "Casual Parties" presents a range of menus for four or more that can be served around the clock. Each menu begins with a practical guide to organizing the meal, including decorating ideas, advance-cooking strategies and beverage recommendations. Recipes in most cases can easily be adapted for larger gatherings.

🌳 Once you've decided to invite people over, browse through the menus in this book, keeping in mind the type of party you desire and your guests' personal tastes, if you know them. Accompanying each menu are suggestions for a range of occasions it suits. The menus are designed to be flexible, so that you can mix and match recipes from one menu to another, too. Variations are offered, as well, so that many recipes can be slightly altered for a whole new flavor.

Setting the Scene

Informal entertaining offers great leeway when deciding where to hold a party, how to set and decorate the table, and the way in which the food is served.

🌳 Let your imagination, as well as the size and layout of your home, dictate where you will present the meal. Your dining room, of course, is an obvious choice. But some gatherings take on a feeling of greater warmth and spontaneity if they are held in a comfortable kitchen or family room. Sunny weather might welcome a move outdoors to a patio or balcony, while a chilly day might steer you toward a fireplace. The mood you are aiming for, as well as the specific recipes and the size of the party, will determine whether you serve the food on individual plates arranged in the kitchen, family style from large bowls and platters at the dining table or buffet style.

🌳 Throughout this book, a variety of dishware, glassware and cutlery is used, each kind chosen to match the occasion and the food or drink being served. Let these selections act only as inspiration for making your own table-setting choices. Work first with what you have, then combine different patterns, or borrow or buy additional pieces. (For a guide to setting a casual table, see pages 186–87.)

🌳 That same spirit of flexibility, ease and appropriateness also applies to your choice of decorations. Gather flowers from the garden or pick them up at a neighborhood florist, then display them in a simple fashion that enhances the scene. (For some creative flower arranging ideas, see pages 188–89.) If you like, add to the mood with your choice of lighting and favorite music.

Putting It All Together

In the end, however, the success of any party depends less on how you set the scene or even on the food or drink you serve than it does on how welcome you make your guests feel. In the belief that a relaxed host or hostess is the best party giver, this book takes the guesswork out of your casual entertaining, which should put you as much at ease as your guests are sure to be.

Casual Dinners

Dinner, more than any other meal, is thought of as ideal for entertaining. While evening generally calls for a more ritualized progression of courses—the appetizer, the main course, side dishes and dessert—than morning or midday repasts, the mood can remain appropriately light and informal, even as the guests linger over conversation and the evening slowly winds down.

The following menus make the most of dinner's informal potential, whether you're welcoming one companion for a quiet candlelit meal or a roomful of friends and relations for a more spirited affair. You will also find menus geared to your time needs, with meals that can be gradually put together over a week or assembled in just an afternoon.

WELCOME HOME DINNER

THE SIMPLE PHRASE "Welcome Home" may do more to warm the heart than any other words. Whether it marks the return of a family member or of a friend, and whether it falls on a special holiday, during a school break or after a long trip, a homecoming dinner delights guests and hosts alike with its informal, generous hospitality.

The style of the party setting matters far less than the spirit with which you stage the event. Whether you invite close friends of the guest of honor or celebrate with just family, bring out your long-cherished dishes and other memorabilia to help rekindle fond memories. This menu, in all its charm and simplicity, would suit almost any close-knit gathering. For our party, we kept the decorations comfortingly casual: flowers grouped in antique containers and baskets and favorite collectibles scattered here and there.

Left uncovered to show off its lovingly worn finish, an old pine table is set with new and old Majolica dishware. Separate plates are set atop the dinner plates for the first-course crab cakes.

Menu

OUR WELCOME HOME menu features recipes that are time-honored favorites: a crab cake appetizer, roast leg of lamb and a rich chocolate dessert.

While carving and serving the lamb with its accompaniments at table may best suit this close-knit occasion, the crab cakes look most attractive presented on individual plates. We suggest serving them from the kitchen. The chocolate mousse torte also looks best brought to the table in individual slices.

Beverage Ideas

This traditional meal demands classic companions. A smoky single-malt scotch before dinner will begin things on the right note. Later, move to an aromatic Sauvignon Blanc, Vernaccia or Semillon to accompany the crab cakes. The lamb calls for a Bordeaux or a California Cabernet Sauvignon. Pour a late-harvest Zinfandel or ruby port with dessert.

Deviled Crab Cakes on Mixed Greens
with Ginger-Citrus Vinaigrette

Roast Leg of Lamb
with Braised Garlic, Sherry & Thyme

Herbed Mashed Potatoes

Glazed Carrots with Grapes & Walnuts

Chocolate Mousse Torte
with Cold Zabaglione Sauce

A bottle of wine brought by a guest is displayed with glasses in an antique wine holder decorated with grapes and a bow.

Preparation List

❧ One day before, assemble the crab cake mixture, form into cakes and coat with bread crumbs; prepare the leg of lamb for roasting and refrigerate.

❧ Up to eight hours before, make the torte and the zabaglione sauce. At the same time, make the vinaigrette and wash and crisp the greens; ready the carrots and grapes for cooking and poach the garlic cloves.

❧ One and one-half hours before, begin to bake the potatoes and roast the lamb.

EACH RECIPE YIELDS 6–8 SERVINGS.

An old ceramic mixing bowl from the kitchen becomes an impromptu vase for snapdragons, ranunculi, freesias and assorted wildflowers.

Deviled Crab Cakes on Mixed Greens with Ginger-Citrus Vinaigrette

SERVES 6–8

Seek out fresh crab meat for these special cakes. They are moist and flavorful but not too spicy. The crab cake mixture can be made the night before and the cakes formed and breaded and then covered and refrigerated. The vinaigrette can be made and the greens washed and crisped 8 hours in advance. Cook the crab cakes just before serving or keep warm in a 300°F (150°C) oven for up to 15 minutes. If you like, use watercress for part of the lettuce and/or garnish the greens with diced avocado or mango (see page 184) and then drizzle with the vinaigrette.

FOR THE CRAB CAKES:

3 tablespoons unsalted butter
1 cup (5 oz/155 g) finely chopped
   yellow onion
⅓ cup (1½ oz/45 g) finely chopped
   celery
¼ cup (1½ oz/45 g) finely chopped
   red or green bell pepper (capsicum)
1 tablespoon dry mustard
½ teaspoon cayenne pepper
1 lb (500 g) fresh crab meat, picked
   over for shell fragments and cartilage
⅓ cup (3 fl oz/80 ml) mayonnaise
1 egg, lightly beaten
½ cup (1 oz/30 g) fresh bread crumbs
1 tablespoon finely grated lemon zest
   (see page 185)
4 tablespoons chopped fresh flat-leaf
   (Italian) parsley
salt and freshly ground pepper
1 cup (4 oz/125 g) fine dried bread
   crumbs

FOR THE GINGER-CITRUS VINAIGRETTE:

¾ cup (6 fl oz/180 ml) peanut oil
finely grated zest of 1 lemon or lime
   (see page 185)
¼ cup (2 fl oz/60 ml) lemon or lime
   juice
2 tablespoons grated, peeled fresh
   ginger
1 fresh jalapeño (hot green) chili pepper,
   seeded, if desired, and minced
sugar
salt

8 cups mixed torn lettuces
peanut oil for frying

To make the crab cakes, in a sauté pan over medium heat, melt the butter. Add the onion and sauté until translucent, about 8 minutes. Add the celery and bell pepper and sauté until tender, about 5 minutes longer. Stir in the mustard and cayenne pepper and cook for 1–2 minutes, stirring constantly to prevent scorching. Transfer to a bowl and let cool completely. Add the crab meat, mayonnaise, egg, fresh bread crumbs, lemon zest and parsley. Fold together gently until all the ingredients are thoroughly incorporated; do not overmix. Season to taste with salt and pepper. Form into 8 cakes each about ½ inch (12 mm) thick.

🌳 Place the dried bread crumbs on a plate or in a shallow bowl and, working with 1 cake at a time, coat the cakes evenly with the crumbs. Cover and refrigerate for at least 1 hour or as long as overnight; the cakes will hold together better if they have been chilled.

🌳 To make the vinaigrette, in a bowl, whisk together the peanut oil, lemon or lime zest and juice, ginger and jalapeño. Season to taste with sugar and salt.

🌳 Toss the lettuces with half of the vinaigrette and divide among the 6–8 individual plates.

🌳 To cook the crab cakes, in a large frying pan over medium-high heat, pour in oil to a depth of 1 inch (2.5 cm). When the oil is shimmery, slip the cakes into the pan, working in batches if the pan is too crowded. Fry, turning once, until golden, 2–3 minutes on each side.

🌳 To serve, place the warm crab cakes atop the greens and drizzle with the remaining vinaigrette. Serve at once.

The occasion's happy informality inspires a whimsical display of family collectibles playing on the theme of coming home to roost.

Deviled Crab Cakes on Mixed Greens with Ginger-Citrus Vinaigrette

Roast Leg of Lamb with Braised Garlic, Sherry & Thyme;   Herbed Mashed Potatoes

Roast Leg of Lamb with Braised Garlic, Sherry & Thyme

SERVES 6–8

The lamb can be roasted with the bone in, or you can ask the butcher to bone the leg and tie it for easier carving and more uniform slices. It is best to insert the garlic and thyme sprigs into the leg the day before roasting to flavor the meat more intensely, but this step can also be done just before the leg goes into the oven. Be sure to remove the lamb from the refrigerator about an hour before putting it in the oven.

1 leg of lamb, about 6 lb (3 kg)
3 or 4 cloves garlic, cut into slivers
12–14 small fresh thyme sprigs, each
  ½ inch (12 mm) long
salt and freshly ground pepper

FOR THE BRAISED GARLIC:
3 heads garlic, cloves separated and
  peeled
beef stock, to cover
3 fresh thyme sprigs
1 bay leaf

FOR THE SAUCE:
beef stock as needed
1 cup (8 fl oz/250 ml) dry sherry
4 teaspoons chopped fresh thyme
salt and freshly ground pepper

Cut 12–14 small, shallow slits into the surface of the lamb. Insert a sliver of garlic and a thyme sprig into each slit. Cover and refrigerate for up to 1 day.
🌳 Preheat an oven to 400°F (200°C). Sprinkle the lamb with salt and pepper and place in a roasting pan.
🌳 Roast for about 1¼ hours for rare with the bone in, or until a meat thermometer registers 130°F (54° C). A boneless leg will take about 1 hour.
🌳 While the lamb is roasting, prepare the braised garlic. In a saucepan over medium heat, combine the garlic cloves, stock to cover barely, thyme sprigs and bay leaf. Cover, bring to a simmer and continue to simmer over medium heat until the garlic is tender when pierced with a fork, about 25 minutes. Remove from the heat and, using a slotted spoon, transfer the garlic to a small bowl. Strain the cooking liquid into a 2-cup (16-fl oz/500-ml) measuring cup.
🌳 To make the sauce, add stock to the strained liquid to measure 2 cups (16 fl oz/500 ml) and transfer to a saucepan. Add the sherry and bring to a boil. Boil, uncovered, over high heat until reduced by one-third. Add the chopped thyme and reserved braised garlic cloves. Adjust the seasoning with salt and pepper and keep warm.
🌳 When the lamb is done, remove from the oven and cover loosely with aluminum foil. Let rest for 10 minutes. Carve the lamb and divide evenly among individual plates. Spoon some of the sauce, including the garlic cloves, over each serving of the lamb. Serve immediately.

Herbed Mashed Potatoes

SERVES 6-8

Who doesn't love mashed potatoes? They are in the true spirit of a casual meal. You can use light cream, heavy cream or milk. And if you like the sharp flavor, butter-milk is lower in fat and will work well, too. The potatoes should be baked on a separate baking sheet. They can be mashed ahead of time and held over warm water until ready to serve.

6 large baking potatoes, about 3 lbs
  (1.5 kg)
1 cup (8 fl oz/250 ml) light (single)
  cream, heavy (double) cream or milk
6 tablespoons (3 oz/90 g) unsalted butter
2 teaspoons chopped fresh parsley
2 teaspoons chopped fresh thyme
2 teaspoons chopped fresh marjoram
salt and freshly ground pepper

Preheat an oven to 400°F (200°C).
🌳 Pierce the potatoes several times with a fork and place them directly on the oven rack or on a baking sheet and bake until very tender, about 1 hour. Remove from the oven and let cool just until they can be handled.
🌳 While the potatoes are cooling, heat the cream in a small saucepan over medium-low heat until small bubbles form at the edge of the pan. Cut the potatoes in half and scoop out the pulp into a bowl. Then pass the pulp through a potato ricer or a food mill placed over a large saucepan. Alternatively, scoop out the pulp into a bowl and mash with a potato masher, then transfer to a large saucepan.
🌳 Add the butter to the potatoes and mash it into them with a spoon or fork. Then, with the saucepan over low heat, gradually add the hot cream to the potatoes, stirring constantly. Continue to stir well until the desired consistency is achieved.
🌳 Mix in the herbs and season to taste with salt and pepper. If you're not ready to serve, transfer potatoes to the top pan of a double boiler or to a heatproof bowl and place over (but not touching) hot water. When ready, transfer to a serving dish and serve immediately.

Glazed Carrots with Grapes & Walnuts

Glazed Carrots with Grapes & Walnuts

SERVES 6–8

The carrots and grapes can be prepared for cooking up to 8 hours in advance. For a citrusy accent, add 2 teaspoons grated lemon or orange zest (see page 185) with the stock. This dish is also good prepared with currants instead of grapes (see below). A sprinkling of chopped fresh mint makes a good garnish.

1 large bunch carrots, peeled and sliced
    about ¼ inch (6 mm) thick (about
    6 cups/1½ lb/750 g)
¼ cup (2 oz/60 g) unsalted butter
1 cup (8 fl oz/250 ml) chicken stock or
    water
3 tablespoons sugar
1 cup (6 oz/185 g) seedless red grapes,
    cut in half
½ cup (2 oz/60 g) chopped walnuts
salt and freshly ground pepper

In a wide sauté pan over high heat, combine the carrots, butter, stock or water and sugar. Bring to a boil, then reduce the heat to medium-low. Simmer, uncovered, until the carrots are tender and the pan juices are reduced to a syrupy glaze, 8–10 minutes.

Stir in the grapes and walnuts and season to taste with salt and pepper. Serve immediately.

Glazed Carrots with Currants and Walnuts

Omit the grapes. In a small bowl, combine 1 cup (6 oz/185 g) dried currants and hot water to cover. Let stand for 20 minutes until plumped, then drain, reserving the soaking liquid. Measure the soaking liquid and use in place of part or all of the stock or water. Add the currants with the walnuts.

To decorate everyday candlesticks, attach grapes, flowers or ivy to your candleholders with florist's tape, then conceal the tape with ribbon.

Chocolate Mousse Torte with Cold Zabaglione Sauce

SERVES 6–8

Utterly rich, this would make a special birthday cake for a chocoholic. The cold zabaglione is a dramatic addition. The torte can be made the day before, but it will taste best if made no more than 8 hours ahead. Serve at room temperature. The sauce can also be spooned over fresh berries or simple pound cake. Served right off the heat, this rich wine custard is called zabaglione *in Italy and* sabayon *in France. It can be chilled for up to 8 hours.*

8 oz (250 g) bittersweet chocolate
1 cup (8 oz/250 g) unsalted butter
1 cup (8 oz/250 g) sugar
¼ cup (2 fl oz/60 ml) brewed coffee
10 eggs, separated
1 teaspoon vanilla extract (essence)
½ cup (2½ oz/75 g) all-purpose
   (plain) flour
½ teaspoon salt

FOR THE ZABAGLIONE:
1 cup (8 fl oz/250 ml) dry Marsala
7 egg yolks
7 tablespoons (3½ oz/105 g) sugar
1 cup (8 fl oz/250 ml) heavy (double)
   cream

2 cups (8 oz/250 g) raspberries or
   strawberries

*P*reheat an oven to 350°F (180°C). Butter the bottom and sides of a 9-inch (23-cm) springform pan, then line the bottom of the pan with parchment paper.

❧ In the top pan of a double boiler or in a heatproof bowl placed over (but not touching) hot water, combine the chocolate, butter, sugar and coffee. Heat until the chocolate and butter are melted, then stir until smooth. Remove from the heat and whisk in the egg yolks and vanilla. Then fold in the flour and salt.

❧ In a bowl, using an electric mixer set on medium speed, beat the egg whites until frothy. Increase the speed to high and beat until medium-firm peaks form. Gently fold the egg whites into the batter just until they fully disappear. Do not overmix. Transfer the batter to the prepared pan.

❧ Bake the torte until it springs back when touched lightly in the center, 45–60 minutes.

❧ While the torte is baking, make the zabaglione. In a bowl, whisk together the Marsala, egg yolks and sugar until well blended. Pour through a fine-mesh sieve into the top pan of a large double boiler or into a large heatproof bowl. Place the pan or bowl over (but not touching) simmering water. Using a whisk or an electric mixer set on medium speed, beat until thickened, pale and fluffy, 10–15 minutes. The mixture should double in volume.

❧ Remove the pan or bowl from the heat and immediately nest in a bowl of ice to cool it down completely. In a chilled bowl with chilled beaters, whip the cream until stiff peaks form. Fold the cold custard into the whipped cream. Cover and refrigerate.

❧ Remove the torte from the oven when done and let cool completely in the pan on a wire rack. Remove the pan sides and transfer the torte to a serving plate. Cut into wedges and serve with the zabaglione sauce and the berries.

Chocolate Mousse Torte with Cold Zabaglione Sauce

AFTER-WORK SUPPER

SOONER OR LATER, an occasion arises when you want to invite colleagues home for a meal, whether to work on an ongoing project, to celebrate a job well done or to make a good impression. The challenge is to prepare and present a delicious meal with minimal effort in the midst of a busy workweek, while also striking the right casual tone.

Because guests may arrive with you from work, or show up soon after, it's a good idea to set the table the night before, using everyday flatware, dishes and napkins on simple place mats. Table decorations can be equally straightforward. We composed the centerpiece the night before by gathering a bunch of forced, flowering bulbs, although any cut flowers that are robust enough to last a few days, such as daisies, ranunculi, Queen Anne's lace or roses, can be purchased in advance and arranged in simple vases.

Previously forced to flower in glass vases, an assortment of white-blossomed bulbs, here, tulips, narcissi, hyacinths, and freesias, was grouped together on the dining table the night before to form an informal centerpiece.

Menu

O̧UR AFTER-WORK menu features Moroccan-style recipes that, while exotic enough to elicit comment, are nonetheless familiar and likely to appeal to everyone. Most of the dishes are prepared largely in advance. Quantities are easily doubled if you want to entertain a larger group of co-workers.

While you look after last-minute details, you might want to offer ice-cold cocktails. The classic martini of gin or vodka and a touch of dry vermouth has experienced a renaissance of late, and may be especially welcomed on a Friday evening as a way to launch the weekend. For nondrinkers, provide sparkling water.

Roasted almonds and marinated olives accompany freshly mixed martinis, prepared in a classic shaker.

Lentil Soup

*White Fish with
Moroccan Spice Marinade*

Couscous

Moroccan Vegetables

Dried Apricot or Melon Compote

Preparation List

❧ Up to three days before, make the dried apricot compote, if serving.

❧ The day before, make the lentil soup up to the point where the greens are added.

❧ The night before, make the fish marinade; prepare the onion base and cook the carrots and cauliflower for the Moroccan vegetables. Cook and chill the melon compote, if serving.

❧ An hour before dinner is served, marinate the fish, cook the couscous and wilt the greens for the soup.

EACH RECIPE YIELDS 4 SERVINGS.

Beverage Ideas

After cocktails (if serving), launch the meal with a glass of spicy and bright Pinot Noir from Oregon or a simple Burgundy or Côtes du Rhône. Stay with the same wine or switch to a crisp Vouvray or German or Pacific Northwest Riesling to accompany the fish. With dessert, serve an Asti Spumante or Muscat-based wine.

A sturdy, woven-raffia mat underscores a place setting with tasteful simplicity. Deep bowls await the lentil soup.

Lentil Soup

SERVES 4, WITH LEFTOVERS

Brown, red or green lentils can all be used in this soup. The green lentils are firmest, so they are best to use if you want to see whole lentils in the soup. The amount of water in which you cook the lentils will vary, depending upon how dry they are; older lentils will require the larger amount. The soup can be prepared the day before and reheated, but wilt and stir in the greens just before serving. A dollop of yogurt or crème fraîche adds a sharpness that cuts some of the richness of the lentils.

2 tablespoons olive oil

1 large yellow onion, diced

1 teaspoon ground cumin

1 large or 2 small carrots, peeled and diced

2 cups (14 oz/440 g) lentils

5–6 cups (40–48 fl oz/1.25–1.5 l) chicken stock or water

2 cups (4 oz/125 g) coarsely chopped spinach, Swiss chard or watercress, carefully washed

salt and freshly ground pepper

plain yogurt or crème fraîche for serving, optional

In a saucepan over medium heat, warm the olive oil. Add the onion and sauté until tender and translucent, about 8 minutes. Add the cumin, carrots, lentils and stock or water and bring to a boil. Reduce the heat to low, cover and simmer until the lentils are soft; begin testing for doneness after 20 minutes.

Meanwhile, in a large sauté pan over medium heat, place the spinach or other greens with just the washing water clinging to the leaves. Cook, turning occasionally, just until wilted. Remove from the heat and drain well.

Stir the greens into the soup. Season to taste with salt and pepper and serve at once, topped with the yogurt or crème fraîche, if desired.

Arrayed on the kitchen counter, choose from an appealing tableau of lentil varieties—(from left) red, green and brown—any of which can be used to make the first-course soup. Green lentils are often labeled "French Green" and may be smaller, denser beans. Regardless of color, the flavor of the lentils will be consistent.

White Fish with Moroccan Spice Marinade

SERVES 4

An easy dish that goes together quickly to produce a wonderfully fragrant and exotic main course. The marinade can be prepared the night before or in the morning and takes just moments to combine. The fish should marinate for at least 40 minutes, but for no more than 1 hour before cooking. It can be baked or broiled, as you like.

FOR THE MARINADE:

2 tablespoons fresh lemon juice

¼ teaspoon saffron threads, steeped in 3 tablespoons warm water for 30 minutes

3 tablespoons chopped fresh flat-leaf (Italian) parsley

3 tablespoons chopped fresh cilantro (fresh coriander)

1–2 cloves garlic, minced

1½ teaspoons paprika

2 teaspoons ground cumin

1 teaspoon freshly ground pepper

⅓ teaspoon ground cinnamon

½ teaspoon ground ginger

1 teaspoon salt

6 tablespoons (3 fl oz/90 ml) olive oil

4 firm white fish fillets such as cod, flounder, northern halibut or swordfish, about 6 oz (185 g) each

olive oil for brushing on fish, if broiling (grilling)

To make the marinade, in a bowl, mix spices with lemon juice and then add olive oil. Arrange the fish fillets in a glass or plastic container and spoon half of the marinade over them. Turn the fillets to coat evenly. Cover and marinate in the refrigerator for at least 40 minutes or for up to 1 hour.

🌳 Preheat an oven to 450°F (230°C), or preheat a broiler (griller). If baking the fish, lightly oil a baking dish large enough to accommodate the fish in a single layer. Place the fillets in the dish and bake until opaque at the center when pierced, about 8 minutes.

🌳 If broiling (grilling), lightly brush the fish fillets on both sides with olive oil and place on a broiler pan. Broil (grill), turning once, until opaque at the center, about 4 minutes on each side.

🌳 Serve the baked or broiled fillets with the remaining marinade spooned over the top.

A selection of pungent spices for the marinade make a fragrant display on a countertop.

Couscous

SERVES 4

A staple of North African cuisine, couscous is the name given to both the tiny pellets made from semolina and to the dish made from them. With the advent of instant couscous, this dish takes but a few minutes to prepare. It can be made up to 1 hour in advance and transferred to the top pan of a double boiler over hot water to keep warm. Or place the baking pan in a warm place. It is important that the couscous puff up fully, so be sure to give it enough time to absorb all of the liquid. The grains will be light and fluffy.

1½ cups (7½ oz/235 g) instant couscous

2¼ cups (18 fl oz/560 ml) water or chicken stock

½ teaspoon salt

1–2 tablespoons unsalted butter or oil, optional

pinch of ground cinnamon, cumin or ginger, optional

Place the couscous in a 1½-qt (1.5-l) baking pan. In a saucepan, bring the water or stock to a boil. Add the salt and the butter or oil and one of the spices, if using. Pour the boiling liquid evenly over the couscous, stir well once and then cover the pan with aluminum foil. Set aside.

🌳 After 10 minutes, remove the foil and fluff the couscous with a fork to separate the grains. Re-cover and keep warm until ready to serve (see note). Fluff again just before serving.

White Fish with Moroccan Spice Marinade; Couscous

Moroccan Vegetables

SERVES 4, WITH LEFTOVERS

Despite the numerous ingredients that go into this dish, it is actually quite easy to prepare and serve. Both the carrots and cauliflower can be parboiled and the seasoned onions prepared the night before. Then all you need to do before serving is reheat the onions and add the vegetables and seasonings. If fresh mint is unavailable, substitute 1 tablespoon dried mint, crumbled, adding it with the carrots and cauliflower to the onion mixture.

2 tablespoons olive oil

1 large yellow onion, diced

½ teaspoon salt

2 cloves garlic, minced

1 teaspoon paprika

½ teaspoon freshly ground black
   pepper

½ teaspoon cayenne pepper, or to taste

1 teaspoon ground ginger

½ teaspoon ground cinnamon

1 cup (8 fl oz/250 ml) chicken or
   vegetable stock or water

6 carrots, peeled and cut into 2-inch
   (5-cm) lengths

1 large cauliflower, cut into florets

2 tablespoons fresh lemon juice

4 tablespoons chopped fresh mint

Moroccan, Kalamata, Sicilian or other
   full-flavored black olives, optional

toasted almonds, optional (see page 185)

In a large sauté pan over medium heat, warm the olive oil. Add the onion and sauté until tender and translucent, about 8 minutes. Add the salt, garlic, paprika, black pepper, cayenne pepper, ginger and cinnamon and sauté, stirring from time to time, for 3 minutes longer. Add the stock or water and simmer for 1–2 minutes. Remove from the heat and set aside.

🌳 Bring a saucepan three-fourths full of salted water to a boil. Add the carrots and boil until tender but still firm, 5–6 minutes. Using a slotted spoon, transfer the carrots to a bowl. Add the cauliflower florets to the same boiling water and boil until tender but still firm, about 5 minutes. Drain well.

🌳 Reheat the onion mixture over medium heat. Add the carrots and cauliflower and toss well to coat with the onion mixture. When the mixture reaches a simmer, cover and heat until warmed to serving temperature. Stir in the lemon juice, then taste and adjust the seasonings.

🌳 To serve, transfer to a serving dish and sprinkle with the mint and with the olives and almonds, if using.

Moroccan Vegetables

Dried Apricot or Melon Compote

SERVES 4

Dried fruits make a wonderful dessert compote in winter. However, in warmer months, you may want to choose a fresh fruit compote to serve with this menu. This recipe gives you a choice.

If you like, a mixture of dried fruits can be used in place of the apricots and raisins in the winter compote. Prepare it up to 3 days ahead of serving. The melon compote can be made up to 24 hours ahead.

FOR THE DRIED APRICOT COMPOTE:

1½ lb (750 g) dried apricots
⅓ cup (2 oz/60 g) golden raisins
5–6 cups (40–48 fl oz/1.25–1.5 l) water, Riesling, Moscato or other sweet wine, to cover
1 cup (8 oz/250 g) sugar, or to taste
2 orange zest strips (see page 185)
½ teaspoon ground cardamom
1–2 tablespoons orange flower water or rose water, or to taste
¾ cup (4 oz/125 g) toasted pine nuts or slivered almonds, optional (see page 185)

☙ In a bowl, combine the apricots, raisins and enough of the water or wine to cover. Let stand overnight at room temperature. The next morning, transfer the fruits and their soaking liquid to a saucepan and add additional water or wine as needed to cover. Add the sugar, orange zest and cardamom and bring to a boil, stirring to dissolve the sugar. Reduce the heat to medium and simmer, uncovered, until the apricots are tender, about 30 minutes.

🌳 Remove fruit from the heat and stir in orange flower water or rose water and nuts, if using. Transfer to a bowl; cool, cover and chill before serving.

FOR THE MELON COMPOTE:

1½ cups (12 fl oz/375 ml) water
¼ cup (2 fl oz/60 ml) fresh lemon juice
1 cup (8 oz/250 g) sugar
orange zest (see page 185)
2–3 lb (1–1.5 kg) cantaloupe or honeydew melon, peeled, seeded and scooped into balls or diced
½ teaspoon ground cardamom
1 tablespoon rose water
chopped pistachios or toasted slivered almonds (see page 185)

☙ In a saucepan, combine water, lemon juice, sugar and orange zest to taste. Bring to a boil while stirring; cook 10 to 15 minutes, or until syrupy. Stir in the melon and the cardamom. Simmer 5 minutes. Remove from heat and stir in rose water. Transfer fruit to a bowl, cool, cover and chill before serving. Garnish with pistachios or almonds.

Dried Apricot Compote, left
Melon Compote, right

AUTUMN
SUNDAY SUPPER

IN THE AUTUMN, as the days grow shorter and the nights turn cooler, people enjoy coming together to share the season's harvest. A casual Sunday supper for family and friends offers the opportunity to enjoy the first glimpses of winter in a warm atmosphere built upon wholesome food and close companionship.

Autumn's early twilight can often carry with it a hint of darkness, so we decided to brighten our table with lively Asian touches, including Japanese stoneware dishes, bamboo-handled cutlery and orchid plants displayed in red lacquerware baskets. It also makes a pleasing contrast to this classically Western menu. Of course, any assortment of accessories in burnished autumn colors will suit the occasion equally well, and such graceful touches as tangerines and fallen leaves only enhance the ambience.

OR THIS MENU suited to a cozy gather-ing of six, we felt a roast chicken would be the ideal centerpiece. Autumnal side dishes include baked yams, a stuffing with seasonal mushrooms and a spiced cranberry sauce flavored with tangerine juice and zest. The chicken could be served on an oversized platter and carved at the table.

For the soup that starts the meal, we used an heirloom tureen. The table was set with soup bowls already in place, each one nestled in a napkin that we folded into a nest (see page 187). Once the guests have finished the soup, the bowls and napkins are cleared away.

Menu

To chase autumn's chill, offer cups or mugs of hot tea soon after guests arrive or at the end of the meal. Green, jasmine or herbal teas, which require no milk, go especially well with the dessert.

Beverage Ideas

Begin with an aperitif of dry sherry or Madeira and follow it with a medium- to full-bodied white (Chardonnay, a Bordeaux Graves or an Australian Semillon). A fragrant medium-bodied red, such as Beaujolais Nouveau, a young Pinot Noir or a Merlot, will marry well with the chicken. End with a pear eau-de-vie chilled or in coffee.

Spinach Soup with
Madeira Cream

Roast Chicken with
Mushroom-Pancetta Stuffing

Cranberry-Tangerine Conserve

Gratin of Yams

Green Beans & Celery

Pear Clafouti

Bamboo, available in art or garden supply shops, can be cut into varying lengths, attached to the sides of votive candles with hot glue and then tied with cord.

Preparation List

❧ Make the conserve well in advance, up to four days ahead of the dinner.

❧ The night before, make the stuffing.

❧ Early in the morning, make the soup up to the point where it is puréed. Prepare the pears for the *clafouti* and place in the baking dish.

❧ Up to four hours before, assemble the gratin and stuff the chicken.

❧ Two hours before, boil the beans, roast the chicken and ready the ingredients for the *clafouti* batter.

❧ Just before sitting down to dinner, assemble and bake the *clafouti*.

EACH RECIPE YIELDS 6 SERVINGS.

An attractive table runner was put together by sewing a band of fabric similar to the napkins around an inexpensive woven beach mat. It can be used again and again.

Spinach Soup with Madeira Cream

SERVES 6

To ensure this soup keeps its bright green color, add the spinach at the last minute and barely wilt it in the stock. Then purée the soup and reheat gently with the cream and wine. The soup can be made up to 8 hours in advance to the point where it is puréed. Finish it just before serving. As an alternative to stirring the cream directly into the soup, whip the cream until soft peaks form, beat the Madeira into it and top each serving with a dollop of the cream.

¼ cup (2 oz/60 g) unsalted butter
2 cups (8 oz/250 g) diced yellow onion
1 baking potato, about 8 oz (250 g),
    peeled and thinly sliced
2 cups (16 fl oz/500 ml) chicken stock,
    plus chicken stock as needed for
    thinning soup
1½–2 lb (10–12 oz) spinach, stems
    removed, carefully washed and
    drained (10–12 firmly packed cups)
1 cup (8 fl oz/250 ml) heavy (double)
    cream
¼ cup (2 fl oz/60 ml) Madeira or dry
    sherry
¼ teaspoon freshly grated nutmeg
salt and freshly ground pepper

In a large, wide saucepan over medium heat, melt the butter. Add the onion and sauté, stirring, until tender and translucent, 8–10 minutes. Add the potato and the 2 cups (16 fl oz/500 ml) chicken stock and bring to a boil. Cover, reduce the heat to low and simmer until the potato is soft, 8–10 minutes.

🌳 Raise the heat to high and start adding the spinach leaves by the handful, pushing them down into the hot stock with a spoon. When all of the spinach has been immersed in the stock, cook until it is barely wilted, 1–2 minutes.

🌳 Working in batches and using a slotted spoon, transfer the soup solids to a blender or food processor fitted with the metal blade and blend or process until smooth; it will be very thick. Pour the purée into a clean saucepan and add the liquid from the original pan.

🌳 Stir in the cream and Madeira or sherry and reheat gently, thinning with additional stock if necessary; do not allow to boil. Season with the nutmeg and salt and pepper to taste. Serve in warmed bowls.

For centerpieces with an Asian simplicity, set orchid plants in decorative containers and surround them with moss.

Spinach Soup with Madeira Cream

Roast Chicken with Mushroom-Pancetta Stuffing

SERVES 6

The stuffing can be made up to 24 hours ahead, or use packaged cubed bread for the stuffing. Stuff the bird and put it in the oven about 2 hours before mealtime.

FOR THE STUFFING:

4 cups (8 oz/250 g) cubed day-old bread (about ½ loaf)

½ cup (4 oz/125 g) unsalted butter

½ lb (250 g) *pancetta,* cut into slices ¼ inch (6 mm) thick and then cut into strips ¼ inch (6 mm) wide

1 cup (4 oz/125 g) diced yellow onion

2 cups (6 oz/185 g) sliced fresh flavorful mushrooms, wild or cultivated, such as chanterelle or portobello

2 teaspoons chopped fresh thyme

2 teaspoons chopped fresh sage

½–¾ cup (4–6 fl oz/125–180 ml) chicken stock

salt and freshly ground pepper

FOR THE CHICKEN:

1 large roasting chicken, about 6 lb (3 kg)

1 lemon, cut in half

salt and freshly ground pepper

paprika, optional

FOR THE BASTE:

½ cup (4 fl oz/125 ml) olive oil

¼ cup (2 fl oz/60 ml) fresh lemon juice

3 cloves garlic, smashed with the side of a knife

1 tablespoon chopped fresh sage

1 teaspoon chopped fresh thyme

1 teaspoon freshly ground pepper

Roast Chicken with Mushroom-Pancetta Stuffing; Cranberry-Tangerine Conserve

To make the stuffing, preheat an oven to 300°F (150°C). Spread the cubed bread in a large rimmed baking sheet and toast in the oven, stirring from time to time, until dried out, about 1 hour.

🌳 Meanwhile, in a large sauté pan over medium heat, melt ¼ cup (2 oz/60 g) of the butter. Add the *pancetta* and sauté until it is nearly crisp, 5–8 minutes. Using a slotted spoon, transfer the *pancetta* to a large bowl and set aside. To the fat remaining in the pan, add the onion and sauté over medium heat until tender and translucent, 8–10 minutes. Transfer the onion to the bowl holding the *pancetta*.

🌳 In the same pan over medium heat, melt the remaining ¼ cup (2 oz/60 g) butter. Add the mushrooms and sauté until they give off some liquid, about 5 minutes. Stir in the thyme and sage. Transfer the mushrooms and their juices to the bowl holding the *pancetta* and onion.

🌳 Add the bread cubes to the bowl and pour ½ cup (4 fl oz/125 ml) of the stock evenly over the top. Toss until all the bread cubes are evenly moistened, adding more stock as needed if the stuffing seems too dry. Season with salt and a generous amount of pepper. Cover and refrigerate for as long as overnight before stuffing the chicken.

🌳 Preheat an oven to 375°F (190°C). Wipe the bird inside and out with a damp cloth and then with a cut lemon. Rub the cavity lightly with a little salt and pepper. Spoon the stuffing loosely into the body and sew or truss closed. (Place any extra stuffing in a buttered baking dish, cover tightly and slip it into the oven with the chicken about 45 minutes before the chicken is done.)

🌳 Place the chicken, breast side down, on a rack in a roasting pan. Sprinkle the flesh with salt, pepper and with a little paprika, if desired.

🌳 To make the baste, in a small bowl, stir together the olive oil, lemon juice, garlic, sage, thyme and pepper.

🌳 Place the chicken in the oven and roast for 45 minutes, brushing or spooning the basting juice over the bird every 15 minutes.

🌳 Turn the chicken, breast side up, and continue to roast, basting every 15 minutes, until tender and juices run clear when a thigh is pierced with a skewer or long fork, 30–45 minutes longer. To test with a roasting thermometer, insert it into the thickest part of the thigh away from the bone; it should register 180°F (82°C).

🌳 Remove from the oven, cover loosely with aluminum foil and let rest for about 15 minutes. Using a spoon, remove the stuffing from the cavity and place in a serving bowl. Carve the chicken and serve immediately.

To better highlight the bright red color of the cranberry conserve, present it in a clear glass bowl or pottery in a bright, contrasting color.

Cranberry-Tangerine Conserve

MAKES ABOUT 6 CUPS (3 LB/1.5 KG)

It doesn't have to be a holiday to serve a tangy cranberry conserve to accompany roast chicken or turkey. Frozen cranberries can be found throughout the year. The conserve can be made up to 4 days in advance, covered and stored in the refrigerator.

finely grated zest of 3–4 tangerines
  (see page 185)
2 cups (16 fl oz/500 ml) fresh tangerine
  juice
1½ cups (12 oz/375 g) sugar
½ teaspoon ground ginger
½ teaspoon ground cinnamon
4 cups (1 lb/500 g) cranberries

In a saucepan over high heat, combine the tangerine zest, 1½ cups (12 fl oz/375 ml) of the tangerine juice, sugar, ginger and cinnamon. Bring to a boil, stirring to dissolve the sugar. Reduce the heat to medium and simmer, uncovered, for 10 minutes. Add the cranberries and cook until the berries pop and the mixture starts to bubble, 5–7 minutes longer.

🌳 Stir in the remaining ½ cup (4 fl oz/125 ml) tangerine juice and continue to simmer, stirring occasionally, until the cranberries are tender and the juices are syrupy but not too thick, 10–15 minutes. The syrup will continue to thicken as the conserve cools.

🌳 Remove from the heat, transfer to a bowl and let cool. Serve at room temperature.

Gratin of Yams

SERVES 6

This delicious cream-free gratin is made with what Americans call yams, although these dark-skinned tubers with deep orange flesh are actually a variety of sweet potato and unrelated to the true yam. Assemble the gratin about 4 hours before serving. Toasted hazelnuts make a nice topping if you are not using almonds on the Green Beans & Celery (see following recipe).

6–9 yams (3 lb/1.5 kg)
½ cup (4 fl oz/125 ml) apple cider
¼ cup (2 fl oz/60 ml) maple syrup
¼ cup (2 oz/60 g) firmly packed
    brown sugar
1 tablespoon fresh lemon juice
½ teaspoon ground ginger or freshly
    grated nutmeg
½ teaspoon ground cinnamon
6 tablespoons (3 oz/90 g) unsalted
    butter
salt
toasted hazelnuts (filberts), peeled and
    chopped, optional (see page 185)

*P*reheat an oven to 375°F (190°C). Butter a large rectangular baking dish or two 9-inch (23-cm) square baking dishes.
🌳 Bring a large saucepan three-fourths full of water to a boil. Add the yams and boil, uncovered, until they can be pierced but are still quite firm, about 30 minutes. Drain, immerse in cool water to stop the cooking and drain again.
🌳 Peel the yams and then slice crosswise ½ inch (12 mm) thick. Arrange the slices in a single layer, overlapping them (or in 2 layers), in the prepared baking dish(es).

Gratin of Yams; Green Beans & Celery

🌳 Meanwhile, in a small saucepan over medium heat, combine the apple cider, maple syrup, brown sugar, lemon juice, ginger or nutmeg and cinnamon. Bring to a boil, stirring to dissolve the sugar, and boil for 10 minutes. Swirl in the butter, then pour the mixture evenly over the yams. Sprinkle lightly with salt and strew toasted hazelnuts (if using) over the top.
🌳 Bake uncovered, basting occasionally with the pan juices, until the yams are tender, 20–25 minutes. Serve immediately from the dish.

Green Beans & Celery

SERVES 6

If you are not topping the yam gratin with hazelnuts, sprinkle almonds over this dish. You can boil the green beans 2–4 hours in advance.

1½–2 lb (750 g–1 kg) green beans,
    trimmed
¼ cup (2 oz/60 g) unsalted butter or
    ¼ cup (2 fl oz/60 ml) olive oil
1 cup (3½ oz/105 g) sliced yellow
    onion

4 large celery stalks, cut on the diagonal
   into strips ¼ inch (6 mm) wide
1 cup (4 oz/125 g) sliced toasted
   almonds, optional (see page 185)
salt and freshly ground pepper

*B*ring a large saucepan three-fourths
full of salted water to a boil. Add the
green beans and boil until tender-crisp,
3–5 minutes. Drain, immerse in ice water
to stop the cooking and drain again. Pat
dry with paper towels and cut into 2-inch
(5-cm) lengths. Set aside.

🌳 In a large sauté pan over medium
heat, melt the butter or warm the oil.
Add the onion and sauté, stirring, until
tender and translucent, 8–10 minutes.
Add the celery, raise the heat slightly and
stir and toss for 3–4 minutes. Add the
green beans and almonds (if using) and
heat to serving temperature. Season to
taste with salt and pepper. Transfer to a
warmed dish and serve immediately.

Pear Clafouti

SERVES 6

A clafouti (also commonly spelled
clafoutis *for both the singular and plural*
forms) is a rustic fruit "pancake" from
France's Limousin region. It is tradition-
ally prepared with cherries, but pears are
a delicious alternative. The fruit can be
arranged in the baking dish 8 hours before
and the batter ingredients measured out up
to 2 hours before. Before sitting down to
dinner, blend the batter ingredients, pour
the batter over the fruit and bake.

1½–2 lb (750 g–1 kg) ripe but firm
   Bosc or Anjou pears, peeled, halved,
   cored and cut into 1-inch (2.5-cm)
   pieces
⅓ cup (3 fl oz/80 ml) pear brandy or

Pear Clafouti

½ cup (4 fl oz/125 ml) sweet white
   wine
3 tablespoons minced candied
   ginger, optional
2 tablespoons unsalted butter
3 eggs
½ cup (2½ oz/75 g) all-purpose (plain)
   flour
½ cup (4 oz/125 g) granulated sugar
½ teaspoon ground cinnamon, optional
1 cup (8 fl oz/250 ml) milk
½ cup (4 fl oz/125 ml) heavy (double)
   cream
finely grated zest of 1 lemon or
   ½ orange (see page 185)
1 teaspoon vanilla extract (essence)
pinch of salt
confectioners' (icing) sugar

*P*reheat an oven to 375°F (190°C). In
a small saucepan over medium heat, mix
the pears, brandy or wine and candied

ginger (if using). Cook gently, stirring
occasionally, until the pears are tender
but not mushy, about 10 minutes.

🌳 Meanwhile, thoroughly grease a
10-inch (25-cm) pie plate or other shallow
round baking dish with the butter. When
the pears are ready, distribute them and
their juices evenly on the bottom of the
prepared pie plate.

🌳 In a blender or in a bowl, blend or
whisk together the eggs, flour, granulated
sugar, cinnamon (if using), milk, cream,
zest, vanilla and salt until well mixed. To
eliminate any lumps, scrape down the
sides of the blender container and blend
the batter again. Let the batter rest for
about 5 minutes.

🌳 Pour the batter evenly over the pears.
Bake until puffed and set, 35–40 minutes.
Remove from the oven and sift a light
dusting of confectioners' sugar over the
top. Serve warm.

DATE DINNER FOR TWO

A FIRST-EVER INVITATION to dinner presents a delicate balancing act. It aims, as it should, to make both a good impression on your guest and to express your interest without fanning the flames of romance too vigorously.

Gracious informality, we believe, is the key, and to that end we decided to place a small table in the living room, setting it with a subtly checked cloth, woven place mats, simple pottery plates and nice tumblers to replace the usual stemmed wineglasses. In the same casual spirit, we chose to arrange pretty but understated bouquets in a simple glass vase and in a tin florist's bucket, and we lit the table with votive candles rather than more formal tapers. A bowl of seasonal fruit and, perhaps, one or two favorite objects make the table for two appear pleasingly personal but not overdone.

If you like, precede the meal with a glass of Champagne or, as shown here, sparkling wine. Two delicate tumblers strike a more casual tone than tall Champagne flutes would.

Menu

Our menu for two impresses subtly by offering courses based on popular but light ingredients: shrimp, chicken breast, white rice and seasonal green beans or asparagus. More important still, it encourages animated conversation with exotic but unintimidating dishes inspired by the cuisines of Asia. A rich chocolate mousse, made special with a hint of orange, provides an appropriately sweet finale.

All of the recipes are easy to prepare and some of the work can even be done up to two days in advance; only brief cooking is required before serving—leaving you free to devote your full attention to your guest.

Beverage Ideas

Start with a half bottle or split of brut Champagne or sparkling wine. Continue with a zesty white with just a snap of sweetness, such as a German or American Riesling. If you prefer a red, try a Beaujolais or an Italian Dolcetto or Barbera. End the meal with an orange Muscat wine or chilled Cointreau.

*Asian-Inspired Shrimp Salad
with Tropical Fruit*

Satay with Peanut Dipping Sauce

Rice Pilaf

*Asparagus or
Green Beans with Ginger*

Chocolate-Orange Mousse

*At each place setting, a shallow glass bowl atop a simple pottery
dinner plate awaits the first-course salad.*

Preparation List

❧ You can make the peanut dipping sauce for the satay a day or two before.

❧ One day before, cube the meat for the satay; peel and cook the shrimp and make the chocolate mousse.

❧ In the morning or during the day, make the vinaigrette and cut up the papaya, mango or cucumber. Wash, dry and crisp the lettuces for the salad.

❧ Three to five hours before, marinate the meat for the satay and trim the asparagus or green beans.

EACH RECIPE YIELDS 2 SERVINGS.

*With little fuss, small
seasonal bouquets may be
arranged with other
attractive mementos to form
a decorative display on a
mantel or sideboard.*

Asian-Inspired Shrimp Salad with Tropical Fruit

SERVES 2

Tangy fruit and opalescent pink shrimp dressed with a spicy sweet-and-tart vinaigrette make a nice light beginning for a special meal. If you cannot find a mango or papaya in the market, 2 oranges, peeled and sectioned, or ½ cantaloupe, peeled, seeded and diced, can be substituted. Or the salad can be made without fruit and with the addition of cucumber (see below). The shrimp can be poached the night before or earlier in the day when you prepare the vinaigrette. Dice or slice the fruit as you like. Assemble at the last minute.

2 cups (16 fl oz/500 ml) water or dry
  white wine
½ lb (250 g) medium-sized shrimp
  (prawns), peeled and deveined
  (about 10)
1 ripe papaya or mango (see page 184)
3 cups (6 oz/185 g) torn mixed lettuces
3 tablespoons torn fresh mint leaves
3 tablespoons torn fresh basil leaves

FOR THE VINAIGRETTE:

⅓ cup (3 fl oz/80 ml) peanut oil or
  olive oil
finely grated zest of 1 lime (see page
  185)
3 tablespoons fresh lime juice
1 tablespoon brown sugar
½ teaspoon red pepper flakes or
  ½ teaspoon diced fresh jalapeño (hot
  green) chili pepper, or to taste
salt

In a saucepan over high heat, bring the water or wine to a boil. Add the shrimp and cook until they turn pink and curl, 3–5 minutes. Using a slotted spoon, transfer to a bowl. Cover and refrigerate until needed.

🌳 If using a papaya, peel, then cut in half lengthwise and scoop out and discard the seeds. Dice or slice the flesh. If using a mango, cut off the flesh from either side of the large central pit, then dice or slice the flesh as shown on page 184. (There will be some tasty flesh still clinging to the pit; eat it off while standing over the sink for a true chef's treat.)

🌳 In a bowl combine the lettuces, mint and basil and toss to mix.

🌳 To make the vinaigrette, in a small bowl, thoroughly whisk together the peanut or olive oil, lime zest and juice, brown sugar, pepper flakes or jalapeño pepper and the salt to taste.

🌳 Add a few tablespoons of the vinaigrette to the shrimp, toss well and let stand for a few minutes. Drizzle half of the remaining vinaigrette over the lettuces and herbs and toss thoroughly. Divide the lettuce mixture between 2 individual plates. Top with the shrimp and papaya or mango. Drizzle the remaining vinaigrette over the top.

Shrimp Salad with Cucumber

Omit the fruit. Peel 1 small cucumber, cut in half lengthwise and scoop out and discard the seeds. Slice the cucumber thinly and place in a bowl. Add 2 tablespoons of the vinaigrette to the cucumber, toss well and let stand for 10 minutes. Proceed as directed for the shrimp and lettuce mixture, then assemble the salad, substituting the cucumber for the fruit.

The key to stress-free cooking is to have all the ingredients assembled beforehand. Here, the components of the dish are readily accessible on a countertop; only the fruit needs last-minute attention.

*Asian-Inspired Shrimp
Salad with Tropical Fruit*

Satay with Peanut Dipping Sauce

SERVES 2

The meat can be cubed the day before and then marinated in the refrigerator 3 to 5 hours in advance or at room temperature for 30 minutes while you assemble the rest of the meal. Lemongrass can be found in Southeast Asian stores and well-stocked food stores. For the coconut cream, purchase a can of coconut milk and, without shaking the can, open it and skim off the thick layer of cream that has settled on the top. The peanut sauce can be made 2 days in advance and reheated. Fruit salsa (recipe on page 182) may be substituted for the peanut sauce if you have prepared the shrimp salad with cucumber rather than fruit.

FOR THE MARINADE:

2 cloves garlic

1 piece fresh ginger, about 1 inch (2.5 cm) long, peeled and sliced

2 tablespoons minced green (spring) onions

2 tablespoons minced lemongrass or 2 teaspoons finely grated lemon zest (see page 185)

2 tablespoons soy sauce

2 tablespoons bourbon, rice wine or dry sherry

1 tablespoon Asian sesame oil

½ teaspoon freshly ground white pepper

CHOICE OF ONE:

4 half chicken breasts, boned and skinned, 4–6 oz (125–185 g) each

2 beef fillet steaks, 6–8 oz (185–250 g) each

2 small pork tenderloins, about 6 oz (185 g) each

FOR THE PEANUT DIPPING SAUCE:

½ cup (5 oz/155 g) unsalted peanut butter

2 tablespoons fresh lemon or lime juice

2 tablespoons coconut cream

¼ cup (2 fl oz/60 ml) water

2 tablespoons soy sauce

¼ teaspoon cayenne pepper, or to taste

½ teaspoon curry powder

sugar

olive oil or peanut oil

salt and freshly ground pepper

To make the marinade, in a food processor fitted with the metal blade or blender, combine the garlic, ginger, green onions and lemongrass or lemon zest. Using on-off pulses, process to form a purée. Add the soy sauce, bourbon or wine, sesame oil and white pepper and process just until blended.

🌿 To make the satay, select one of the meats and cut into 1-inch (2.5-cm) cubes. Place in a glass or plastic container, add the marinade and toss to distribute evenly. Cover and refrigerate for 3–5 hours, turning occasionally, or marinate at room temperature for 30 minutes.

🌿 To make the dipping sauce, in a heavy saucepan over medium heat, combine the peanut butter, lemon or lime juice, coconut cream, water, soy sauce, cayenne pepper, curry powder and sugar to taste. Bring to a simmer, stirring constantly. Transfer to the top pan of a double boiler or to a heatproof bowl and place over (but not touching) hot water until serving.

🌿 Preheat a broiler (griller), or make a fire in a charcoal grill. Soak 6 bamboo skewers in water to cover for about 15–30 minutes.

🌿 Drain and thread the meat cubes onto the soaked skewers. Brush the meat with olive or peanut oil and sprinkle with salt and pepper to taste.

🌿 Place the skewers on an oiled grill and grill, turning once, until cooked, 2–3 minutes on each side for chicken or beef and 4–5 minutes on each side for the pork. Serve with the warm dipping sauce.

Peanut butter, coconut cream, citrus juice, soy sauce, spices and sugar meld their flavors to make a Southeast Asian–style peanut sauce.

Satay with Peanut Dipping Sauce

Rice Pilaf

SERVES 2

Here is a classic rice pilaf that may be embellished with any number of additions. If you are serving the peanut sauce with the satay, do not top the pilaf with toasted nuts. Do not use the currants if you are serving the fruit salsa with the satay.

2 tablespoons peanut oil or olive oil
1 small yellow onion, diced (4–5 tablespoons/1½ oz/45 g)
1 cup (7 oz/220 g) basmati or jasmine rice, rinsed and drained
2 cups (16 fl oz/500 ml) water or chicken stock
1 piece fresh ginger, about 1 inch (2.5 cm) long, peeled and smashed
salt

SUGGESTED ADDITIONS:
2 tablespoons toasted pine nuts or almonds (see page 185)
2 tablespoons dried currants, plumped in hot water to cover for 20 minutes and drained
3 tablespoons minced green (spring) onions, green tops only
1 small ripe tomato, peeled, seeded and diced
2 tablespoons flaked coconut, lightly toasted in a dry frying pan

In a saucepan over medium heat, warm the peanut or olive oil. Add the onion and sauté until translucent, about 8 minutes. Add the rice and sauté for a few minutes until the kernels are thoroughly coated with the oil.

🌳 Add the water or stock, ginger and salt to taste and bring to a boil. Cook for 2 minutes, reduce the heat to low, cover and simmer until the water is absorbed, 15–20 minutes.

🌳 Stir in the additions of choice and remove from the heat. Let rest for 10 minutes, then fluff with a fork, remove ginger and serve at once.

Asparagus or Green Beans with Ginger

SERVES 2

A green vegetable is the perfect accompaniment to the satay and rice. The asparagus or green beans can be readied 3–5 hours in advance. Asparagus are most flavorful when still crisp, while green beans taste best when they are cooked until somewhat tender. You can also use spinach (see variaton at right) in place of the asparagus or green beans.

10 oz (315 g) asparagus or green beans
2 tablespoons peanut or vegetable oil or unsalted butter
¼ cup (1½ oz/45 g) minced yellow onion
1 tablespoon grated, peeled fresh ginger (see page 185) or ½ teaspoon red pepper flakes
1 teaspoon minced garlic
⅔ cup (5 fl oz/160 ml) water or chicken or vegetable stock
finely grated zest of 1 lemon (see page 185) or fresh lemon juice, optional
salt and freshly ground pepper

If using the asparagus, break off the ends, where they snap easily. Peel the stalks with a paring knife or vegetable peeler if they are thick. Cut on the diagonal into 2-inch (5-cm) lengths. If using the green beans, trim off their tops and tails and cut in half crosswise if they are longer than 2 inches (5 cm).

🌳 In a sauté pan over medium heat, warm the peanut or vegetable oil or melt the butter. Add the onion and sauté until tender, about 5 minutes. Add the ginger or pepper flakes and garlic and sauté, stirring often, for 2 minutes longer. Add the water or stock and the beans or asparagus and cook, uncovered, over medium heat until the vegetables are tender and have absorbed most of the water or stock, 5–6 minutes for the beans and about 4 minutes for the asparagus.

🌳 Stir in the lemon zest or juice to taste, if using, and then season to taste with salt and pepper. Serve immediately.

Spinach with Ginger
Carefully wash 1 lb (500 g) spinach and trim off the stems. Sauté the onion, ginger and garlic as directed, then add the spinach with its washing water still clinging to its leaves. Omit the ⅔ cup (5 fl oz/160 ml) water or stock. Cook uncovered as directed, turning the spinach occasionally with a fork, just until wilted and tender, 3-5 minutes. Season as directed.

Rice Pilaf; Asparagus with Ginger

Chocolate-Orange Mousse

SERVES 2, WITH LEFTOVERS

This is an ideal dessert for two, as it can be prepared fully the night before and poured into individual ramekins ready for serving. The recipe makes about two or three 1-cup (8 fl oz/250 ml) portions, depending upon how much air you whip into the egg whites and cream. But it is so good you may not mind having an extra serving on hand. Look for high-quality candied orange peel in food-specialty stores.

2 oz (60 g) semisweet chocolate

2 tablespoons fresh orange juice or
   orange-flavored liqueur

2 eggs, separated

pinch of salt

¼ cup (2 oz/60 g) sugar

½ cup (4 fl oz/125 ml) heavy (double)
   cream

2 teaspoons minced candied orange
   peel, optional

Combine the chocolate and orange juice or liqueur in the top pan of a double boiler or in a heatproof bowl. Place over (but not touching) simmering water and stir until melted and smooth. Remove the pan or bowl from over the water and let cool a bit, then whisk in the egg yolks until well blended.

In a bowl combine the egg whites and salt. Using an electric mixer, beat until soft peaks form. Gradually add the sugar, continuing to beat until stiff, but not dry, peaks form. Stir one-third of the beaten whites into the melted chocolate to lighten it, and then gently fold in the remaining whites into the mixture.

In a chilled bowl with chilled beaters, beat the cream until stiff peaks form. Gently fold the cream into the chocolate mixture.

Divide the mixture evenly among 2 or 3 attractive ramekins. Cover and refrigerate until set, at least 2 hours or for up to 1 day.

To serve, garnish with the candied orange peel, if desired.

Gourmet coffee shops now sell a variety of sweeter roasts that go especially well with dessert. Serve freshly brewed regular or decaffeinated coffee and offer Muscat wine or an orange-flavored liqueur, such as Cointreau.

Chocolate-Orange Mousse

DINNER WITH DEAR FRIENDS

HEN BEST FRIENDS come to dinner, as we hope they often do, there's no need to prepare an elaborate feast. Whether you are celebrating a reunion, memories of a shared vacation or no occasion at all, a simple yet delicious meal offers the opportunity to relax a little and enjoy one another's company.

We decided to serve this sit-down dinner in an informal dining room setting. It would be equally appropriate to set it in a family room, or even in the kitchen, if large enough. We opted for everyday table accessories: a straw runner and mats, celadon dishware, bistro-style flatware and stemless glasses. Indeed, every item here might already be on your shelf, making this style of party ideal for a spontaneous get-together, whoever your guests might be.

Batik napkins add a touch of the tropics to casual dinnerware. Votive candles nestled within glass hurricane shades shed a soft, warm light.

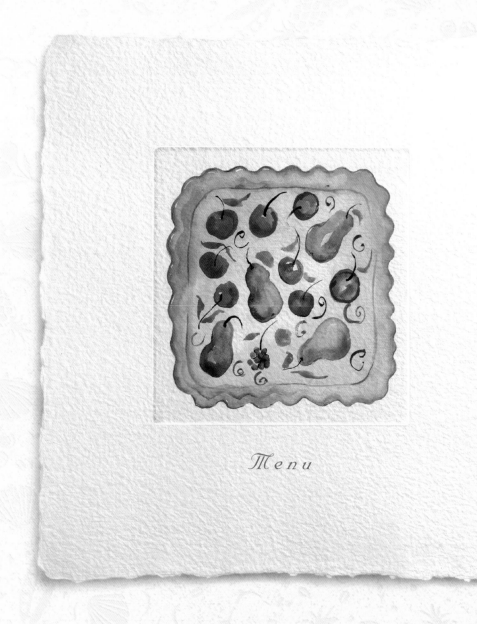

Menu

Our MENU FOR special friends features a main course that couldn't be more homey: beef stew, with potatoes and a big green salad, followed by an old-fashioned crisp made with seasonal fruit. Yet, you'll find sophisticated-but-easy touches in each of these recipes that make the cozy gathering feel extra special.

The first course is a variation on the Scandinavian-style, home-cured salmon known as gravlax. If you don't have the time to prepare this dish you can substitute good-quality, store-bought gravlax or smoked salmon, serving it with the mustard sauce, cucumber and pumpernickel suggested on page 63.

Let your friends help themselves from an old-fashioned dry bar arranged on a tray or side table. Provide assorted glasses, napkins, a bucket of ice, a pitcher of water and the spirits and mixers that you know from experience they'll like.

Gravlax with Mustard Sauce

◆

Beef Stew

Creamless Potato Gratin

Green Salad with
Gruyère & Croutons

◆

Fruit Crisp

Preparation List

❧ Four or five days before, make the gravlax and assemble and freeze the streusel topping for the crisp.

❧ Marinate the meat for the stew the night before you plan to cook it.

❧ The day before the dinner, cook the stew and make the mustard sauce.

❧ Four hours before, make the fruit crisp, vinaigrette and croutons; wash and crisp the lettuces and slice the potatoes for the gratin.

EACH RECIPE YIELDS 6 SERVINGS.

Beverage Ideas

Select a full-bodied American or Australian Chardonnay or an Alsatian white wine to accompany the gravlax. Pour an elegant Bordeaux, a Napa Valley Cabernet Sauvignon or a luscious Merlot from New York or Washington State to go with the stew. Open a tangy Italian Moscato or lush late-harvest wine to complement the fruit crisp.

For easy table decorations, group together any small, green houseplants you may have or buy some ferns or palms and repot them in containers, using a little Spanish moss to hide their soil.

Gravlax with Mustard Sauce

SERVES 6, WITH LEFTOVERS

It is too difficult to cure a small piece of fish and then slice it neatly. Therefore, it is best to use a 2–3-pound (1–1.5-kg) whole salmon fillet and have some leftovers for sandwiches, brunch or a nice first course for another occasion. The salmon must be cured 4 or 5 days before you plan to serve it. The mustard sauce can be made 1 day in advance. Gin and mint create a particularly light and delicate gravlax with a bold pink color. If you like, substitute aquavit for the gin and the mint for a more traditional gravlax.

1 whole salmon fillet, 2–3 lb (1–1.5 kg), with skin intact

¼ cup (2 oz/60 g) sugar

3 tablespoons kosher salt

½ teaspoon freshly ground pepper

1 tablespoon ground juniper berries

2 teaspoons ground coriander

½ teaspoon ground allspice

zest of 2 small lemons, cut into strips 2 inches (5 cm) long and ¼ inch (6 mm) wide (see page 185)

3 large fresh mint sprigs

3 tablespoons gin

FOR THE MUSTARD SAUCE:

¼ cup (2 oz/60 g) Dijon mustard

1 teaspoon dry mustard

3 tablespoons sugar

2 tablespoons white wine vinegar

½ cup (4 fl oz/125 ml) peanut oil

3 tablespoons chopped fresh mint

1 large English (hothouse) cucumber, peeled, halved lengthwise, seeded and thinly sliced

thinly sliced pumpernickel bread

*P*lace the fish fillet skin-side down in a glass or plastic container. In a small bowl, stir together the sugar, salt, pepper, juniper, coriander and allspice. Rub this mixture evenly onto the flesh side of the fish. Cover the fish with the lemon zest strips and the mint. Sprinkle with gin.

🌲 Cover the fish with plastic wrap. Place a board or tray directly on the fish and then weight the fish with 2 bricks or other heavy weights.

🌲 Chill for 4 or 5 days, basting the fish daily with the juices that accumulate. Remove the weights on the last day.

🌲 To make the sauce, in a food processor or blender, combine the Dijon mustard, dry mustard, sugar and vinegar. Pulse just to combine. Slowly add the peanut oil in a thin, steady stream, processing until the mixture thickens. Alternatively, in a small bowl, whisk together the mustards, sugar and vinegar. Then gradually whisk in the peanut oil until thickened. Fold in the mint.

🌲 To serve, slice the gravlax across the grain at an angle and away from the skin into paper-thin slices. Arrange on a serving plate or individual plates, with the cucumber and pumpernickel. Pass the mustard sauce.

Gravlax with Mustard Sauce

Gravlax takes its name from the Swedish "gravad lax," meaning "buried salmon," which describes the curing technique in its most primitive form. In modern kitchens, the salmon fillet is simply cured and weighted in a glass or plastic container.

Beef Stew

SERVES 6

This old-fashioned beef stew is cooked in the oven, but it can also be simmered on the stove top (see below). The choice of vegetables is also up to you. To give the stew a Greek accent, add currants and cinnamon (see below). Marinate the stew meat overnight (two nights before) and then cook the stew a day before serving. Put it on to cook slowly; the tantalizing aroma will tell you when it's done. Just before serving, reheat on the stove top.

3 lb (1.5 kg) boneless lean stewing beef, cut in 2-inch (5-cm) cubes

FOR THE MARINADE:

4 cups (32 fl oz/1 l) dry red wine
3 yellow onions, quartered
2 bay leaves
3 fresh thyme sprigs
1 fresh rosemary sprig
12 peppercorns
3 whole cloves
6 cloves garlic, smashed with the side of a knife
2 wide orange zest strips (see page 185)

1 can (28 oz/875 g) plum (Roma) tomatoes, seeded and chopped, with their juices
1 lb (500 g) carrots, peeled and cut into 2-inch (5-cm) lengths
1 lb (500 g) fresh mushrooms, halved if large
water or beef stock, as needed
1 cup (5 oz/155 g) black olives, pitted (optional)
salt and freshly ground pepper
chopped fresh flat-leaf (Italian) parsley

Beef Stew; Creamless Potato Gratin

Place the beef in a glass or plastic container. To make the marinade, in a bowl, stir together the red wine, onions, bay leaves, thyme and rosemary sprigs, peppercorns, cloves, garlic and orange zest. Pour the marinade evenly over the meat, turning the meat to coat well. Cover and refrigerate overnight.

Preheat an oven to 400°F (200°C). Drain the beef, reserving the marinade, then strain the marinade through a sieve into a bowl. Remove the herbs, orange zest strips and spices from the sieve and place on a square of cheesecloth (muslin). Bring the corners together and tie to form a small bag. Retrieve the onions and garlic from the sieve and place in a large, heavy ovenproof pan with a tight-fitting lid. Add the beef, tomatoes, carrots and mushrooms.

Add the strained marinade and the spice bag. If the meat is not covered completely by the wine, add water or stock to cover. Cover tightly and place in the oven. When the stew reaches a boil, reduce the heat to 275°–300°F (135°–150°C). Cook until the meat is very tender, about 3 hours.

Remove from the oven and skim off any excess fat. If using the olives, stir them in and allow to heat through. Season to taste with salt and pepper and sprinkle with parsley.

Stove-Top Variation

To cook the stew on the stove top, drain the beef, strain the marinade, make a spice bag and reserve the marinade ingredients as directed. Dry the beef well. Coat with all-purpose (plain) flour that has been seasoned with salt and pepper. In a large sauté pan over medium-high heat, warm 1–2 tablespoons olive oil. Working in batches, brown the beef on all sides, about 10 minutes. Transfer it to a large, heavy pan with a tight-fitting lid. Add the onions, garlic, tomatoes, mushrooms, strained marinade, spice bag and additional water or stock as needed to cover the meat completely. Bring to a boil over high heat, cover, reduce the heat to low and simmer until tender, 2½–3 hours. Add the olives and heat through. Season with salt and pepper. Sprinkle with parsley and serve.

Greek-Style Beef Stew

Prepare the stew as directed, but omit the mushrooms and the olives. About 1 hour before the stew is ready, stir in 1 cup (6 oz/185 g) dried currants and 1 teaspoon ground cinnamon.

Marinating chunks of stewing beef overnight in red wine with onion, orange zest, herbs and spices gives them a rich flavor and tender texture.

Creamless Potato Gratin

SERVES 6

You need not feel guilty when eating this flavorful low-calorie gratin. An alternative to the traditional gratin that is loaded with butter and cream, this gratin has such good flavor you may never make it the old way again. If you prefer to omit the broiler step, sprinkle the cheese over the potatoes before they go into the oven: it will melt and form a nicely browned crust. The potatoes can be sliced up to 4 hours before dinner and kept in water until you assemble the gratin.

3–4 cups (24–32 fl oz/750 ml–1 l) chicken stock or beef stock
salt and freshly ground pepper
6 long white new potatoes, peeled and sliced crosswise ¼ inch (6 mm) thick
½ cup (2 oz/60 g) freshly grated Parmesan or Gruyère cheese

Preheat an oven to 375°F (190°C). Butter a 3-qt (3-l) shallow rectangular or oval baking dish.

Pour the stock into a saucepan and bring to a boil. Season to taste with salt and pepper. Lay the potato slices in the prepared dish. Pour the hot stock evenly over the potatoes to cover barely. Cover tightly with aluminum foil.

Bake until the liquid is absorbed and the potatoes are tender when pierced with a fork, about 40 minutes.

Meanwhile, preheat a broiler (griller). Sprinkle the cheese evenly over the potatoes and slip under the broiler. Broil (grill) until the cheese melts, about 2 minutes. Serve at once.

Green Salad with Gruyère & Croutons

Green Salad with Gruyère & Croutons

SERVES 6

The vinaigrette, croutons and lettuces can be prepared about 4 hours before dinner.

FOR THE HERB VINAIGRETTE:

⅔ cup (5 fl oz/160 ml) mild olive oil

⅓ cup (3 fl oz/80 ml) fruity virgin
    olive oil

¼ cup (2 fl oz/60 ml) Champagne,
    white wine or sherry vinegar

salt and freshly ground pepper

1 teaspoon chopped fresh tarragon,
    chervil or chives

FOR THE CROUTONS:

18–24 baguette slices, each about
    ⅛ inch (3 mm) thick, about ½ loaf

mild olive oil

1–2 cloves garlic

FOR THE SALAD:

about 12 cups (1½ lb/750 g) torn
    mixed lettuces, carefully washed
    and dried

5 oz (155 g) Gruyère cheese, cut into
    thin strips 1½–2 inches (4–5 cm)
    long and ⅛ inch (3 mm) wide
    (about 1 cup)

*P*reheat an oven to 350°F (180°C).

🌳 To make the vinaigrette, in a bowl, whisk together the mild and fruity olive oils, wine or vinegar, salt and pepper to taste and the tarragon, chervil or chives. Set aside.

🌳 To make the croutons, place the baguette slices on a baking sheet. Brush them with olive oil and bake until crisp and golden, 10–15 minutes. Remove from the oven and, while still warm, rub each crouton with a garlic clove.

🌳 To serve, place the lettuces in a large salad bowl. Add the cheese strips and croutons. Drizzle the vinaigrette over the top, toss well and serve at once.

Fruit Crisp

SERVES 6

Bake the crisp 4 hours in advance. The streusel topping can be frozen for up to 5 days. Serve with vanilla ice cream.

FOR THE STREUSEL TOPPING:

1 cup (8 oz/250 g) unsalted butter, at room temperature

½ cup (3½ oz/105 g) firmly packed brown sugar

½ cup (4 oz/125 g) granulated sugar

1⅔ cups (8½ oz/265 g) all-purpose (plain) flour

⅔ teaspoon baking powder

½ teaspoon ground cinnamon

½ teaspoon ground ginger

1 cup (4 oz/125 g) chopped walnuts or almonds, lightly toasted (see page 185)

FOR THE FILLING:

½ cup (2½ oz/75 g) all-purpose (plain) flour

pinch of salt

1–1½ cups (7–10½ oz/220–330 g) firmly packed brown sugar

8 cups (2–3 lb/1–1.5 kg) sliced fruit or whole berries

1 tablespoon vanilla extract (essence)

2 tablespoons finely grated orange or lemon zest (see page 185)

2 tablespoons brandy, Calvados, kirsch or other complementary spirit

To make the streusel, in a bowl, beat the butter and sugars with an electric mixer set on medium until light and fluffy. Reduce the speed and gradually add the flour, baking powder and spices, beating until crumbly. Add the nuts and set aside.

🌳 Preheat an oven to 350°F (180°C). Butter a 9-inch (23-cm) round baking dish or 2-qt (2-l) oval gratin dish.

🌳 To make the filling, in a large bowl, combine the flour, salt and brown sugar, adjusting the amount of sugar depending upon the sweetness of the fruit. Add the fruit, vanilla, citrus zest and brandy or other spirit; toss to mix well. Transfer to the prepared dish.

🌳 Scatter the streusel over the top. (If the streusel is frozen, place it in a food processor fitted with the metal blade and, using on-off pulses, process until the mixture is crumbly.)

🌳 Bake until the top is golden brown and the fruit bubbles up along the edges of the dish, 25–40 minutes, depending upon the type of fruit.

Fruit Crisp

TREE-TRIMMING SUPPER

"IT'S TIME TO come and decorate the tree!" is an eagerly anticipated call when close family members are gathered together for the holiday celebration. Because trimming the tree can often be a major project, it makes sense to simplify the other elements of the gathering. We decided a meal served buffet style on the kitchen counter would be the easiest, letting family members help themselves and eat either in the kitchen or beside the tree.

To emphasize the spirit of the season, build a blazing fire. If your home lacks a fireplace, arrange large candles around the room, taking care, of course, to keep them clear of decorations and wrappings. We dressed our tree with natural ornaments, including pinecones and potpourri sachets, as well as fresh fruit, popcorn garlands and cookies.

A Douglas fir wears natural holiday adornments, such as pinecones and lemons tied on with long raffia strips and florist's wire. Cookies, iced to resemble stained-glass windows, make unusual ornaments.

Menu

THIS MENU FOR six can easily be doubled if you have a big family or if you want to invite guests to join in your celebration. The recipes allow much of the preparation to be done in advance. If you don't have time to bake the bread, buy a loaf from a good local bakery. Set out the pasta and salad in large bowls, with plates or bowls stacked alongside. The dessert can be served later on a tray by the fire.

Beverage Ideas

An herbaceous red wine, medium-full in body and rustic in style, is the perfect match for both the occasion and the dinner. Try an Australian Shiraz, California Zinfandel, tasty French Rhône or an Italian Chianti, Barbaresco or Valpolicella. A ruby port pairs perfectly with the *budino*.

*Pappardelle
with Mushroom Sauce*

Caesar Salad

Rosemary Bread

*Mascarpone Budino
with Sun-Dried Cranberry Compote*

Variegated holly, pine boughs and other evergreen foliage from the garden or the florist are bound together with florist's wire to make a casual holiday wreath in an unusual square shape.

Preparation List

❦ Two or three days before, cook the cranberry compote.

❦ One or two days before, make the starter for the rosemary bread.

❦ Toast the croutons for the Caesar salad and make the *budino* one day before.

❦ That day, bake the bread and make the *pappardelle*. Wash and crisp the lettuce.

❦ An hour before, make the mushroom sauce and the Caesar salad dressing.

EACH RECIPE YIELDS 6 SERVINGS.

An attractive wooden caddy holds casual cutlery for diners to help themselves.

Pappardelle with Mushroom Sauce

SERVES 6

Nothing is quite so satisfying as a bowl of steaming pasta cloaked in a delectable sauce. If you are making the pappardelle, *which are ribbon noodles about 1 inch (2.5 cm) wide, the dough can be mixed and the noodles cut up to 8 hours in advance of cooking. If you do not have time to make the pasta, purchase good-quality fresh* pappardelle. *If you prefer a narrower noodle, make or purchase fresh fettuccine.*

For the sauce, select an assortment of fresh mushrooms—chanterelles, porcini, crimini, portobellos and shiitakes. Even dried porcini can be used: Soak them first in hot water just to cover for about 1 hour, drain, squeeze dry and strain the soaking liquid through a sieve lined with cheese-cloth (muslin). Chop the mushrooms and add them with the herbs; use the strained liquid in place of the stock. The sauce can be made up to 1 hour before serving and then reheated while you cook the pasta.

homemade pasta (recipe on page 181)
 or 1½ lb (750 g) purchased fresh
 pappardelle or fettuccine
3 tablespoons unsalted butter
3 tablespoons olive oil
½ lb (250 g) *pancetta,* sliced ¼ inch (6
 mm) thick, then cut into long
 strips ¼ inch (6 mm) wide, optional
3 yellow onions, sliced ⅛ inch
 (3 mm) thick

2 lb (1 kg) mixed fresh mushrooms,
 sliced ¼ inch (6 mm) thick or left
 whole or halved if small (see note)
about ½ cup (4 fl oz/125 ml) beef,
 chicken or vegetable stock, if needed
2 tablespoons chopped fresh sage or
 thyme
1½ tablespoons minced garlic
salt and freshly ground pepper
freshly grated Parmesan cheese

*I*f you are making the pasta, mix and roll out the dough as directed in the recipe and then cut into strips 1 inch (2.5 cm) wide to form *pappardelle.*

🌳 In a large sauté pan over medium heat, warm 1 tablespoon each of the butter and olive oil. If using the *pancetta,* add it to the pan and sauté, stirring occasionally, until lightly browned, 2–3 minutes. Add the onions and sauté, stirring occasionally, until almost tender, 7–8 minutes longer. Transfer to a bowl and set aside.

🌳 Add 1 tablespoon each butter and olive oil to the same pan over high heat. When the butter melts and is hot, add half of the mushrooms and sauté just until they begin to release their liquid and soften; the timing will depend upon the variety of mushrooms. Transfer to the bowl holding the onions.

🌳 Warm the remaining 1 tablespoon each butter and oil in the same pan. Add the remaining mushrooms and sauté in the same manner. Return the mushroom-onion mixture to the sauté pan and reheat over high heat. If the mixture

A wide selection of mushrooms are now commercially grown and sold in good-quality produce shops (clockwise from top): shiitakes, crimini, chanterelles and portobellos.

seems dry, add as much of the stock as needed to moisten it. Then stir in the sage or thyme and the garlic and sauté, stirring often, for 2 minutes. Season to taste with salt and pepper. Keep warm.

🌳 Meanwhile, bring a large pot three-fourths full of salted water to a boil. When the sauce is ready, drop the pasta into the boiling water and cook, stirring to separate the strands, until al dente, 1–2 minutes. Drain and transfer to a warmed serving platter. Add the sauce, toss gently and serve immediately. Pass the Parmesan cheese.

Caesar Salad

SERVES 6

This is probably the most popular salad in America after plain mixed greens. If possible, use salt-packed anchovies, as they have better flavor. Lightly rinse off the excess salt and remove any small bones before chopping. Buy young, tender romaine heads; reserve any large leaves for another purpose. A fruity olive oil and fresh lemon juice are necessary, as romaine is quite mild in flavor. The croutons can be made the night before. The lettuce can be washed and chilled up to 8 hours in advance of serving. The dressing can be prepared 1 hour before the meal.

FOR THE CROUTONS:

18 baguette slices, each about ⅛ inch (3 mm) thick, about ½ loaf
olive oil
1–2 cloves garlic

FOR THE SALAD:

3 eggs
3–4 tablespoons finely chopped anchovy fillets (see note)
6 tablespoons (3 fl oz/90 ml) fresh lemon juice
¾ cup (6 fl oz/180 ml) virgin olive oil
1 tablespoon minced garlic
4–6 tablespoons (1–1½ oz/30–45 g) freshly grated Parmesan cheese
freshly ground pepper
4–6 small heads romaine (cos) lettuce

To make the croutons, preheat an oven to 350°F (180°C). Arrange the bread in a single layer on a baking sheet. Brush the tops of the slices with olive oil. Bake until crisp and golden, 8–10 minutes. Remove from the oven. Cut the garlic cloves in half. While the bread slices are still warm, rub the toasted slices with the cut side of a clove. Let cool. Alternatively, cut the baguette into ½-inch (12-mm) cubes instead of slices. Smash the garlic cloves. In a large sauté pan over medium heat, warm 4 tablespoons olive oil with the garlic. When the oil is hot, add the bread cubes and toss in the oil until crisp and golden, about 5 minutes.

To make the salad, bring a small saucepan three-fourths full of water to a boil. Working quickly, lower each egg into the boiling water on a spoon. Allow the eggs to remain in the water for 1 minute, then transfer to a bowl of cold water to cool completely.

In a bowl, mash the anchovies with the lemon juice. Break the eggs and add them to the bowl, along with the olive oil, minced garlic and 3 tablespoons of the Parmesan cheese. Whisk together until all the ingredients are fully incorporated. Season to taste with pepper.

Tear the romaine leaves into large bite-sized pieces and place in a large salad bowl. Add the croutons and the dressing and toss to coat the leaves evenly.

Transfer to individual plates and sprinkle with the remaining Parmesan cheese. Serve at once.

Rosemary Bread

MAKES TWO 1½-LB (750-G) LOAVES

This rosemary-flecked loaf is a wonderful accompaniment to the pasta and salad. The recipe yields two loaves, more than you will need for dinner. Use the second loaf for sandwiches or serve at another meal. The starter must be made the night before you plan to bake the bread. It will impart more flavor, however, if it is refrigerated for 1–2 days before using. This recipe yields more starter than you will need for the rosemary loaves. Use the leftover starter for making additional loaves, for other bread recipes or discard it after 1 week.

FOR THE STARTER:

1 cup (8 fl oz/250 ml) tepid water
¼ teaspoon active dry yeast
2 cups (10 oz/315 g) unbleached all-purpose (plain) flour

FOR THE DOUGH:

2 tablespoons active dry yeast
½ cup (8 oz/250 g) starter
2 cups (16 fl oz/500 ml) warm (110°F/43°C) water
3 tablespoons olive oil
2–3 tablespoons chopped fresh rosemary
2 teaspoons salt
3–4 cups (15–20 oz/470–625 g) unbleached all-purpose (plain) flour

To make the starter, in the bowl of an electric mixer fitted with a paddle attachment, combine all the ingredients. Beat at medium speed until the mixture pulls away from the sides of the bowl, about 3 minutes. Alternatively, place all the starter ingredients in a bowl and beat with a wooden spoon until the mixture pulls away from the sides of the bowl. Transfer the starter to a 2-qt (2-l) plastic container that will allow the starter to triple in volume.

Cover and leave at room temperature overnight or refrigerate for 1–2 days before using. You will have about 2½ cups (1¼ lb/625 g).

To make the dough in a heavy-duty electric mixer fitted with the paddle attachment, combine the yeast, starter and warm water in the bowl. Beat until the water is chalky white and foamy, about 5 minutes. Change to the dough hook and add the olive oil, rosemary, salt and 3 cups (15 oz/470 g) of the flour. Beat on medium speed until the dough pulls away from the sides of the bowl, adding up to 1 cup (5 oz/155 g) additional flour if the dough is too soft. Continue to knead with the dough hook until the dough is smooth and elastic, about 10 minutes.

🌳 To make the dough by hand, in a bowl and using a wooden spoon, beat together the yeast, starter and warm water until the water is chalky. Add the olive oil, rosemary, salt and 3 cups (15 oz/470 g) of the flour and beat until well combined and the dough pulls away from the sides of the bowl, adding more flour if the dough is too sticky. Turn out the dough onto a lightly floured board. Knead by hand until smooth and elastic, about 10 minutes, adding more flour as needed to prevent sticking.

🌳 Shape the dough into a ball, place in a lightly oiled bowl, and turn the dough to coat all surfaces with the oil. Cover with a dampened kitchen towel or plastic wrap and let rise in a warm, draft-free place until tripled in size, 1½–2 hours.

🌳 Punch down the dough and divide in half. Shape each half into a free-form loaf and place on a baking sheet. Cover with a towel and let rise until doubled in size, 45–60 minutes.

🌳 Preheat an oven to 425°F (220°C). Make 4 shallow diagonal slashes in the top of each loaf. Bake until golden brown and the bottom of each loaf sounds hollow when tapped, about 45 minutes. Let cool on wire racks.

Caesar Salad; Rosemary Bread

Mascarpone Budino with Sun-Dried Cranberry Compote

SERVES 6

Budino is the Italian term for pudding. This dessert is not only endearing, but it is also positively addictive. It is delicious eaten plain or topped with an orange-scented compote of sun-dried cranberries. Mascarpone, a buttery, creamy cheese, can be found in specialty-food shops and fine food stores. The compote can be made 2–3 days in advance and reheated over medium-low heat until warmed through. The budino can be made the day before serving.

FOR THE BUDINO:

1 lb (500 g) *mascarpone* cheese at
   room temperature
3 eggs
6 tablespoons (3 oz/90 g) sugar
¼ teaspoon almond extract (essence)
1 teaspoon finely grated orange zest (see
   page 185)

FOR THE COMPOTE:

1 cup (4 oz/125 g) sun-dried cranberries
1 teaspoon minced orange zest
   (see page 185)
1 cup (8 fl oz/250 g) fresh orange juice
½ cup (4 oz/125 g) sugar

Preheat an oven to 250°F (120°C).

🌳 To make the *budino,* in a bowl, whisk together the cheese, eggs, sugar, almond extract and zest until well mixed. Strain the mixture through a fine-mesh sieve into a pitcher to remove any lumps. Then divide the mixture among six ½-cup (4-fl oz/ 125-ml) ramekins. Place the ramekins in a large baking pan and pour in hot water to reach halfway up the sides of the ramekins. Cover the baking pan with aluminum foil.

🌳 Place in the oven and bake until the puddings are set along the edge but still quivery in the center, 35–40 minutes. Remove the puddings from the oven and then remove them from the baking pan. Let cool, cover and refrigerate until fully chilled.

🌳 To make the compote, in a small saucepan, combine the cranberries, orange zest and juice and sugar. Place over medium heat and bring to a simmer, stirring to dissolve the sugar.

🌳 Reduce the heat to very low and continue to simmer uncovered, stirring occasionally, until the juice reduces to a thin syrup and the cranberries are tender, about 1 hour.

🌳 Serve the chilled puddings with the warm compote spooned over the top.

An open area close to the tree, such as this French country bench in a corner of the room, can be used to set out a selection of do-it-yourself decorations to trim the tree. A large grape-picker's basket holds an assortment of foliage, including boxwood and holly, ready to fashion into garlands and wreaths. A smaller basket holds freshly popped corn, to be strung into ropes with needle and thread. Small fresh fruits, preferably with stem and leaves attached, can be secured to the tree with lengths of florist's wire. Bow-shaped sachets filled with potpourri are tied on with raffia—a rustic counterpoint to their satiny fabric.

Mascarpone Budino with Sun-Dried Cranberry Compote

AFTER THE HOLIDAYS

HOLIDAYS USUALLY FIND many friends and acquaintances gathered around the dining table. The days after the holidays, however, are best reserved for close family and friends with whom you can comfortably share a meal composed of the best leftovers from the more formal feast.

We chose to prepare this post-holiday meal after Thanksgiving, but you could also use the recipes to follow any holiday or other special dinner that yields up a meaty turkey carcass. Just as we made thrifty use of the turkey, we also employed leftover holiday decorations—in this case, colorful autumn squashes—in a casual table arrangement. If space allows, you might set the table in the kitchen for a more relaxed and easy atmosphere.

ECOGNIZING THAT leftovers can only go so far, and that you probably don't want another houseful of guests so soon after the big holiday meal, the following menu will serve just four people. It is easily made, but it does call for you to prepare a stock from the turkey carcass up to two days ahead of time (although chicken broth can be substituted). The risotto in which the turkey and stock are featured requires regular watching and stirring, so, if guests offer to help, you might let them literally lend you a hand.

Other likely leftovers that find their way into the meal include broccoli and olives, marinated here in a well-seasoned vinaigrette, and pumpkin, which is transformed into a comforting oven-baked flan. Don't worry if you don't have leftovers to incorporate, just make the entire meal from scratch. With the dessert and coffee, you might also serve a plate of simple cookies such as gingersnaps (recipe on page 101) or your favorite sugar cookie.

Menu

Beverage Ideas

Start with a medium-bodied herbaceous French Chablis, Mâcon-Villages or Sancerre; an American Chardonnay or an Italian Pinot Grigio. Change to a mild Italian Chianti, Rosso di Montalcino or Dolcetto; a Spanish Rioja or an American Merlot to drink with the risotto. Finish with tawny port, cream sherry or hot buttered rum.

Assorted Crostini & Toppings

*Broccoli & Olives
with Garlic & Pepper Vinaigrette*

Broiled Stuffed Radicchio

Turkey Risotto

Caramelized Pumpkin Flan

Plaid ribbon borders sewn on checkerboard cotton squares make distinctive seasonal napkins. Wheat sheaves tied with twine could be used to mark each place.

Preparation List

❧ Make the tapenade, pesto and sun-dried tomato spread up to one week before.

❧ Prepare the turkey stock a day or two before the dinner.

❧ The day before, make the flan.

❧ In the morning, blanch and stuff the radicchio and make the vinaigrette.

❧ Two to four hours before, trim, cook and chill the broccoli.

EACH RECIPE YIELDS 4 SERVINGS.

Seasonal decorations such as gourds, squashes and Indian corn provide a varied palette of colors and shapes from which to compose arrangements that will brighten any shelf or table-top in the house.

Set out sliced country bread, cheese and crocks of pesto, tapenade and sun-dried tomato spread and let guests help in the assembly of the crostini.

Assorted Crostini & Toppings

SERVES 4

You can use a baguette or a coarse-textured country-style French or Italian loaf to make the crostini. This colorful first course goes together quickly when the pesto, tapenade and sun-dried tomato spread are in your pantry.

about ½ French baguette or 1 loaf
   country-style French or Italian bread
¼ cup (2 fl oz/60 ml) pesto (recipe on
   page 183)
¼ cup (2 fl oz/60 ml) tapenade
   (recipe on page 182)
¼ cup (2 fl oz/60 ml) sun-dried
   tomato spread (recipe on page 182)
24 small or 12 large slices mozzarella or
   Fontina cheese

*P*reheat a broiler (griller). Cut the baguette into 24 slices each about ¼ inch (6 mm) thick. If using a country-style loaf, cut 12 slices each about ¼ inch (6 mm) thick. Arrange the bread slices on a baking sheet and broil (grill), turning once, until lightly golden, about 2 minutes on each side. Remove from the broiler but leave the broiler on.

🌳 If using baguette slices, spread 8 toasted bread slices with an equal amount of the pesto. If using the larger bread slices, divide the pesto evenly among 4 slices. Then divide the tapenade and the sun-dried tomato spread evenly among the remaining toasted bread slices. Place a cheese slice on top of each, using the size that matches the bread slices.

🌳 Return to the broiler and broil until the cheese melts. Serve immediately.

Assorted Crostini & Toppings

Broccoli & Olives with Garlic & Pepper Vinaigrette

SERVES 4

The spicy-hot vinaigrette is also good on cooked cauliflower or zucchini. It can be made 4–6 hours in advance of combining with the broccoli. The broccoli can be trimmed, cooked and chilled 2–4 hours before serving.

1 large or 2 small heads broccoli, about 1½ lb (750 g) total weight, cut into florets with stems intact and thick stems peeled
½ cup (4 fl oz/125 ml) olive oil
2 teaspoons red pepper flakes
2 tablespoons red wine vinegar
2 cloves garlic, minced
salt and freshly ground pepper
1 cup (5 oz/155 g) Gaeta or similar black olives

*B*ring a large pot three-fourths full of salted water to a boil. Add the broccoli and cook until tender-crisp, 3–4 minutes. Drain, being careful not to break the florets, and immediately immerse in ice water to stop the cooking and preserve the vibrant color. Drain well again and pat dry with paper towels. Cover and chill.

🌳 In a small saucepan over medium heat, warm the olive oil until it is very hot but not smoking. Drop in the pepper flakes and heat until the oil is red, about 30 seconds. Remove the oil from the heat and let cool. Strain through a fine-mesh sieve into a cup with a spout. Stir in the vinegar and garlic and season to taste with salt and ground pepper.

🌳 Just before serving, arrange the chilled broccoli on a platter. Drizzle with the vinaigrette and sprinkle with the olives. Serve immediately.

Broiled Stuffed Radicchio

SERVES 4

The radicchio may be blanched and stuffed up to 8 hours in advance of serving, then basted with olive oil and balsamic vinegar and slipped under a preheated broiler at the last minute. Or, instead of broiling the radicchio, place the stuffed heads in an oiled baking dish, spoon the oil-and-vinegar mixture over them and bake in a preheated 400°F (200°C) oven until tender and browned, about 20 minutes.

4 small heads radicchio, or 2 large heads radicchio, cut in half
⅓ lb (5 oz/155 g) mozzarella, cut into 4 equal pieces
¼ cup (2 fl oz/60 ml) olive oil
2 tablespoons balsamic vinegar
salt and freshly ground pepper

*B*ring a large pot three-fourths full of salted water to a boil. Drop the radicchio heads into the boiling water and cook, pushing the heads under the water when they rise above it, for 2 minutes. Drain well and, when cool enough to handle, carefully but thoroughly squeeze out the excess moisture.

🌳 Preheat a broiler (griller). Carefully pull open the heads of radicchio and tuck a piece of mozzarella into the center of each one. Return the leaves to their original position, overlapping the leaves so that the cheese is covered completely.

🌳 In a small cup, whisk together the olive oil and vinegar. Place the radicchio heads on a broiler pan and sprinkle with salt and pepper. Brush the heads with half of the oil-and-vinegar mixture.

🌳 Broil (grill) for 3 minutes. Turn the heads over and brush with the remaining oil-and-vinegar mixture. Broil until the heads are nicely browned, about 3 minutes longer. Serve immediately.

Hardy seasonal flowers left over from the holiday celebration can do double duty as additional decorations for the post-holiday table by recutting and combining with leaves and wheat.

Broccoli & Olives with Garlic & Pepper Vinaigrette; Broiled Stuffed Radicchio

Turkey Risotto

Turkey Risotto

SERVES 4

Don't throw away that holiday turkey carcass! Trim off all the remaining meat and make a rich stock with the bones, then use the meat and some of the stock to make this delicious risotto. The stock can be made up to 2 days in advance.

For making risotto, you must use a short-grain Italian rice such as Arborio. This is a versatile recipe. A number of suggested additions are included; you can add as few or as many as you like.

FOR THE RISOTTO:

about 5–6 cups (40–48 fl oz/1.25–1.5 l) turkey stock (recipe on page 183) or chicken stock

2 tablespoons olive oil or unsalted butter

½ cup (2½ oz/75 g) minced yellow onion

1½ cups (10½ oz/330 g) imported Italian rice (see note)

2 cups (12 oz/375 g) diced cooked turkey (1-inch/2.5-cm dice)

1 teaspoon chopped fresh sage or 2 teaspoons chopped fresh thyme

SUGGESTED ADDITIONS:

1 cup (5 oz/155 g) shelled fresh or thawed frozen peas

2 cups (6 oz/185 g) sliced fresh mushrooms, sautéed in 1 tablespoon unsalted butter or olive oil until tender

¼ cup (1½ oz/45 g) finely diced prosciutto

1 bulb fennel, trimmed and finely diced

½ cup (4 fl oz/125 ml) dry Marsala

TO FINISH THE RISOTTO:

salt and freshly ground pepper

⅓ cup (1½ oz/45 g) diced Fontina cheese (¼-inch/6-mm dice) or ¼ cup (1 oz/30 g) freshly grated Parmesan cheese, optional

chopped fresh fennel fronds, optional

minced fresh Italian (flat-leaf) parsley, optional

To make the risotto, pour the stock into a saucepan over medium heat and bring to a boil. Reduce the heat to keep the stock at a very low simmer. In a large, wide, deep sauté pan over medium heat, warm the oil or melt the butter. Add the onion and sauté, stirring often, until tender and translucent, 8–10 minutes. Add the rice and stir until it is well coated with the fat, about 2–3 minutes.

🌲 Reduce the heat to low and add about 1 cup (8 fl oz/250 ml) of the simmering stock. Cook, stirring occasionally, until the stock is absorbed, 3–5 minutes. Add another 1 cup (8 fl oz/250 ml) stock and cook, stirring occasionally, until absorbed. Continue to add the stock in this manner, never adding more stock until the previous batch has been absorbed. Continue to cook, stirring occasionally, until nearly all of the liquid is absorbed, the rice is tender but still al dente in the center and the mixture is creamy. It may not be necessary to add all of the stock to achieve this consistency. When you add the final cup of stock, add the turkey and the sage or thyme and stir in as many of the suggested additions—peas, mushrooms and their cooking juices, prosciutto, diced fennel, Marsala—as you like.

🌲 Season the risotto with salt and pepper and stir in the Fontina cheese (if using). Spoon into warmed individual bowls and, if desired, sprinkle with the Parmesan cheese, fennel fronds or parsley. Serve immediately.

In the casual spirit of the occasion, a plate of assorted crostini stems the guests' and the cook's hunger while the risotto is being prepared.

Caramelized Pumpkin Flan

SERVES 4

A good way to use leftover pumpkin, this classic dessert is easy to prepare and best when made the day before serving. Mashed cooked sweet potatoes can be used in place of the pumpkin. If you want a simpler dessert with this menu, the dried apricot compote on page 35 can be served in place of the flan.

¾ cup (6 oz/185 g) sugar
1½ tablespoons water
¾ cup (6 fl oz/180 ml) light (single) cream
½ cup (4 oz/125 g) pumpkin purée
finely grated zest of 1 small orange (see page 185)
½ teaspoon ground cinnamon
pinch of freshly grated nutmeg
¼ teaspoon ground ginger
pinch of salt
2 eggs, lightly beaten
½ teaspoon vanilla extract (essence)

If you wish, accompany the flan with simple cookies, cut into seasonal shapes.

Preheat an oven to 325°F (165°C). In a small saucepan over low heat, combine ½ cup (4 oz/125 g) of the sugar and the water, stirring until the sugar dissolves. Raise the heat to high and cook without stirring until the liquid is caramel colored and has a faintly burnt aroma, 6–8 minutes; do not allow it to burn. Remove from the heat and pour carefully into the bottom of four ½-cup (4 oz/125-ml) custard cups or ceramic ramekins, tilting them to coat the bottoms and sides. Set aside.

🌳 In a saucepan over medium heat, warm the cream until tiny bubbles form along the edge of the pan; do not allow to boil. Meanwhile, in a bowl, combine the pumpkin, the remaining ¼ cup (2 oz/60 g) sugar, orange zest, cinnamon, nutmeg, ginger and salt. Stir to mix well, then stir in the eggs. Gradually stir in the hot cream, a little at a time, and then the vanilla. Stir until smooth and pour into the prepared ramekins. Place the ramekins in a baking pan and pour hot water into the pan to reach halfway up the sides of the ramekins. Cover the pan with aluminum foil.

🌳 Bake until set and a knife inserted in the center of a flan comes out clean, about 45 minutes. Remove from the water bath and let rest on a wire rack for about 30 minutes. Then cover the ramekins and chill well.

🌳 At serving time, run a knife around the inside edge of each ramekin and invert each flan onto a plate or shallow bowl. Serve at once.

Caramelized Pumpkin Flan

SOUP SUPPER
BY THE FIRE

WINTER'S CHILLIEST DAYS bring out the natural desire to gather together beside the fire, seeking warmth in close companionship and good food. Any room that has a fireplace will do. If you don't have a fireplace, cozy seating and enough assorted votives and other candles to cast a warming glow will be just as inviting.

In this casual setting, a coffee table can become both the buffet and, for those seated close to it, the dining table. For other guests, an assortment of small end tables or folding trays within reach would do. A mantel is the perfect place to add seasonal decorations. Here, an arrangement of ivy, branches and moss is embellished with such serendipitous touches as early daffodils, urns of dried yarrow, a bird's nest and a wild porcini mushroom, freshly picked.

For a touch of springtime in midwinter, grow a variety of salad greens from seed indoors in individual glazed pots. Set on a sunny windowsill or in another bright location.

Menu

A HEARTY SOUP IS the ideal main course for a supper by the fire. Our zesty seafood chowder offers great leeway in the choice of ingredients—you can even turn it into a chicken chowder. Ladle it from a tureen, or serve it directly from the pot set on a trivet on the table, into deep bowls, mugs or—as we did—Italian *caffè latte* cups with saucers.

Accompanying the chowder is an array of other dishes, from which guests can choose: freshly baked breadsticks, a tossed salad and a selection of cheeses. Baked apples and ginger-snaps are a tasty, old-fashioned conclusion.

A choice of wines is set out with glasses on a sideboard or table. Through-out the meal guests can pour whichever vintage they prefer.

Seafood Chowder

*Green Salad with Cucumbers,
Walnuts & Mustard-Shallot Vinaigrette*

Sesame Breadsticks

Assorted Cheeses

Baked Apples

Gingersnaps

Preparation List

❧ A couple of days before, bake the ginger-snaps and store in an airtight container.

❧ In the morning, bake the breadsticks and the apples; prepare the base for the chowder through the point at which the potatoes are half-cooked. Make the vinaigrette.

❧ A few hours ahead, wash and crisp the salad greens; toast the walnuts for the salad.

EACH RECIPE YIELDS 6 SERVINGS.

Offset by a folded napkin, a plain glass bowl shows off a baked apple—garnished here with a mint leaf—in all its homey simplicity. An underplate allows gingersnaps to be served alongside.

Beverage Ideas

Despite the chill outside, white wines are best for this menu. Provide a medium-bodied, fragrant young Sauvignon Blanc or Chardonnay. A snifter of good brandy or Calvados will complement the flavors of the baked apples and gingersnaps.

Seafood Chowder

SERVES 6

This Latin American–inspired chowder is versatile and easy to prepare. Use firm, white-fleshed fish, such as cod, snapper, halibut, angler, flounder or sea bass. A variety of shellfish can also be added, including shelled clams, shrimp (prawns) and scallops. If you cannot find fresh baby lima beans, more mature fresh limas can be used; they will need to be blanched for 2–3 minutes in boiling water and then drained before adding to the chowder. Prepare the soup base and half-cook the potatoes in it up to 8 hours in advance. At serving time, simply bring the soup base to a simmer and add the corn, limas and fish or fish and shellfish. Directions for transforming this soup into a chicken chowder follow.

3 tablespoons olive oil

2 yellow onions, chopped

3 cloves garlic, minced

1 tablespoon grated, peeled fresh ginger (see page 185)

finely grated zest of 1 lime or lemon (see page 185)

1 tablespoon paprika

3 celery stalks, chopped

4 tomatoes, peeled, seeded and diced

2 fresh jalapeño (hot green) chili peppers, seeded, if desired, and minced

6 cups (48 fl oz/1.5 l) fish stock or chicken stock

2 cups (10 oz/315 g) diced, peeled potatoes

1 cup (6 oz/185 g) fresh or thawed frozen corn kernels

1 cup (5 oz/155 g) fresh or thawed frozen baby lima beans

1 cup (8 fl oz/250 ml) half-and-half or heavy (double) cream, optional

2 lb (1 kg) assorted firm white fish fillets, cut into spoon-sized chunks, or a mixture of fish fillets and shellfish (see note)

salt and freshly ground pepper

3 tablespoons chopped fresh cilantro (fresh coriander)

*I*n a large, deep saucepan over medium heat, warm the olive oil. Add the onions and sauté, stirring, until tender and translucent, about 8 minutes. Add the garlic, ginger, lime or lemon zest and paprika and sauté for 2 minutes. Then add the celery, tomatoes and jalapeños and sauté for 2 minutes longer.

Add the stock and potatoes and bring to a boil. Reduce the heat to medium and simmer, uncovered, until the potatoes are about half-cooked, 10–12 minutes.

Add the corn, lima beans, half-and-half or cream (if using) and fish or fish and shellfish and simmer, uncovered, until just cooked, about 5 minutes; do not overcook or the seafood will toughen. Season to taste with salt and pepper and sprinkle with the cilantro. Serve at once.

Chicken Chowder

Omit the fish or fish and shellfish and use chicken stock instead of fish stock. Add 6 whole chicken breasts, skinned, boned and cut into 1-inch (2.5-cm) chunks, with the corn and lima beans. Simmer until the chicken is opaque and cooked through, 5–7 minutes.

Seafood Chowder

Green Salad with Cucumbers, Walnuts & Mustard-Shallot Vinaigrette

SERVES 6

This full-flavored vinaigrette coats the salad greens and adds a little zip to the crunchy but bland cucumbers. You can make the vinaigrette early in the day and toast the walnuts and wash and crisp the greens a few hours ahead of supper time. Then it's just toss and serve.

9 cups (9 oz/280 g) mixed torn salad
   greens, including romaine (cos),
   butter lettuces and watercress
2 cucumbers, peeled, seeded and diced
   (about 4 cups/1¼ lb/625 g)
1½ cups (6 oz/185 g) toasted walnuts
   (see page 185)
3 tablespoons chopped fresh dill,
   optional

FOR THE MUSTARD-SHALLOT VINAIGRETTE:

2 tablespoons Dijon mustard
3 tablespoons red wine vinegar
½ cup (4 fl oz/125 ml) mild olive oil
¼ cup (1¼ oz/37 g) minced shallots
salt and freshly ground pepper

In a large salad bowl, combine the salad greens, cucumbers, walnuts and the dill, if using.

🌳 To make the vinaigrette, in a small bowl, whisk together the mustard and vinegar. Gradually whisk in the olive oil until the mixture emulsifies. Stir in the shallots and salt and pepper to taste. Drizzle the vinaigrette over the salad, toss well and serve at once.

For the best, most varied selection of cheeses in peak serving condition, seek out a good-quality food store cheese department, specialty cheese store or delicatessen. Shown here (clockwise from top left): blue cheese, sharp Cheddar, Danish Fontina, herb-coated goat cheese, striped Cheddar-and-blue Huntsman, and a black-peppercorn–flavored Havarti.

Green Salad with Cucumbers, Walnuts & Mustard-Shallot Vinaigrette

Sesame Breadsticks

MAKES ABOUT 1 DOZEN

These fat breadsticks are crisp on the outside and a little chewy on the inside. They can be made even stouter—sort of slim baguettes—and you will end up with only about half as many breadsticks. The dough can be mixed in an electric mixer with paddle and dough hook attachments or by hand. The breadsticks can be made 8 hours in advance and then warmed in a 350°F (180°C) oven just before serving. An equal amount of poppy seeds can be used in place of the sesame seeds.

4 teaspoons active dry yeast

2 tablespoons sugar

½ cup (4 fl oz/125 ml) lukewarm (110°F/43°C) water

⅔ cup (5 fl oz/160 ml) milk

2 tablespoons unsalted butter

3½ cups (17½ oz/545 g) all-purpose (plain) flour

1 teaspoon salt

1 egg

2–3 tablespoons cold water

¼ cup (1 oz/30 g) sesame seeds

In a small bowl, combine the yeast, sugar and the warm water and let stand until creamy, about 5 minutes.

🌳 Meanwhile, in a small saucepan over medium heat, warm the milk until small bubbles appear along the edges of the pan. Add the butter to the milk, immediately remove from the heat and let cool to lukewarm.

🌳 To make the dough in a heavy-duty electric mixer fitted with the paddle attachment, sift together the flour and salt into the mixer bowl. Add the yeast

A few basic ingredients—and a few leisurely hours for mixing, rising, shaping and baking— yield fresh-from-the-oven breadsticks.

mixture to the lukewarm milk, then gradually add the milk-yeast mixture to the flour mixture, beating with the paddle attachment just until a soft dough forms that pulls away from the sides of the bowl, about 5 minutes. Change to the dough hook and knead on medium speed until the dough is smooth and elastic, about 8 minutes.

🌳 To make the dough by hand, prepare and combine the dry yeast and lukewarm milk as directed above. Meanwhile, sift together the flour and salt into a large bowl. Using a large wooden spoon, gradually beat the milk-yeast mixture into the flour mixture until a soft dough forms that pulls away from the sides of the bowl. Turn the bread dough out onto a floured work surface and knead until dough feels smooth and elastic, about 7–10 minutes.

🌳 Shape the dough into a ball, place in a lightly oiled bowl and turn the dough to coat all surfaces with the oil. Cover with a dampened towel or plastic wrap and let stand in a warm, draft-free place until doubled in size, about 1½ hours.

🌳 Preheat an oven to 425°F (220°C). Line 2 baking sheets with parchment paper or oil the sheets.

🌳 Punch down the dough and turn out onto a floured work surface. Divide the dough into 12 equal pieces. Flour your hands and, using your palms, roll each piece on the work surface into a log about 10 inches (25 cm) long. Transfer the shaped breadsticks to the prepared baking sheets. Cover with a dampened towel and let rise in a warm, draft-free place until doubled in size, about 30 minutes.

🌳 In a small bowl, lightly beat the egg with the cold water. Brush the egg mixture on the breadsticks, then sprinkle with the sesame seeds.

🌳 Slip the baking sheets into the oven and mist the breadsticks with a spray mister. Bake until the breadsticks just begin to color, 7–10 minutes, misting the breadsticks about 5 more times during this period. Then reduce the oven temperature to 350°F (180°C) and continue to bake the breadsticks until they are golden brown and sound hollow when tapped on the bottom, about 20 minutes longer. Transfer to wire racks to cool.

Sesame Breadsticks

Baked Apples

SERVES 6

Few other desserts fill the house with such a wonderful fragrance as they cook. Look for Rome Beauty apples at your market, as they are the best for baking. The apples will hold their shape but will also become nice and custardy inside. If you like, serve them with a dollop of cream, crème fraîche, sweetened yogurt or vanilla ice cream. They can be baked up to 8 hours before serving and served at room temperature. Or, if you prefer, warm them in a 350°F (180°C) oven for 15 minutes.

6 large Rome Beauty apples
finely grated zest of 1 orange
   (see page 185)
6 tablespoons (2 oz/60 g) chopped
   raisins
¼ cup (2 oz/60 g) firmly packed
   brown sugar
¼ cup (2 oz/60 g) unsalted butter at
   room temperature
1 teaspoon ground cinnamon
¼ cup (3 oz/90 g) honey
½ cup (4 fl oz/125 ml) fresh orange
   juice or apple cider

Preheat an oven to 350°F (180°C).

🌲 Core the apples to within ½ inch (12 mm) of the base. Then peel them only halfway down from the top. Place side by side in a baking dish.

🌲 In a small bowl, stir together the orange zest, raisins, brown sugar, butter and cinnamon until well mixed. Divide this mixture evenly among the apples, pushing it down into the apple cavities.

🌲 In a small saucepan over medium-low heat, combine the honey and orange juice or cider and heat just until the honey dissolves. Pour the honey mixture evenly over the apples and bake, basting often with the pan juices, until the apples are tender when pierced with a fork, about 45 minutes.

🌲 To serve, let cool to room temperature. Place on individual plates and spoon the pan juices over the top.

Gingersnaps

MAKES ABOUT 4 DOZEN

Crisp ginger cookies are the ideal accompaniment to baked apples. They can be baked up to 2 days in advance of serving and stored in an airtight container at room temperature. Leftover cookies can then be stored for up to 2 days. Here the cookie dough is made with a hand-held mixer, but a stationary mixer fitted with a paddle attachment will make it go together even more easily. Or, of course, you can also beat together all the ingredients with a sturdy spoon.

1 cup minus 1 tablespoon (7½ oz/235 g)
   unsalted butter at room temperature
1¼ cups (10 oz/315 g) sugar
1 extra-large egg
½ cup (4 fl oz/125 ml) dark molasses
2½ cups (12½ oz/390 g) all-purpose
   (plain) flour
2½ teaspoons baking soda (sodium
   bicarbonate)
½ teaspoon salt
2 tablespoons ground ginger
2 tablespoons minced candied ginger
1¼ cups (5 oz/155 g) toasted pecan
   halves, coarsely chopped (see page 185)

In a large bowl, combine the butter and sugar. Using an electric mixer set on medium speed, beat until the mixture is fluffy and light. Add the egg and continue to beat on medium speed until fully incorporated, then beat in the molasses.

🌲 In another, smaller bowl, sift together the flour, baking soda, salt and ground ginger. With the mixer set on low speed, beat the flour mixture into the butter mixture, one third at a time, beating well after each addition. Stir in the candied ginger and pecans.

🌲 Turn the dough out onto a lightly floured work surface. Knead briefly, then divide into 2 equal portions. Using your palms, roll each dough portion into a log 1¼–1½ inches (3–4 cm) in diameter. Wrap each log separately in plastic wrap and refrigerate until well chilled, about 2 hours.

🌲 Preheat an oven to 325°F (165°C). Line 2 baking sheets with standard parchment paper.

🌲 On a lightly floured work surface, slice the dough logs crosswise ⅛ inch (3 mm) thick. Place the dough rounds 1 inch (2.5 cm) apart on the prepared baking sheets.

🌲 Bake until golden, 8–10 minutes. Set on a wire rack to cool completely.

Casual Parties

No matter what the time of day or the season of the year, there's always a reason to throw a casual party—from a housewarming to an engagement shower, an outdoor cookout celebrating summer to a Sunday morning brunch, a weekend card party to a beer-and-pizza extravaganza where everyone lends the cook a hand.

As varied as they are, all the menus that follow share at least one characteristic: In food and decorations alike, they allow everyone to relax and have a good time regardless of the size of the guest list. With a little planning and advance preparation, any one of these festive get-togethers will be as fun for the host as it is for the party goer.

KITCHEN
BREAKFAST

$\mathcal{A}$S CHILDREN, WE are all taught that a good breakfast is the best way to launch the day. That homespun truth has been adopted by hosts and hostesses who know that a generous morning meal served to weekend houseguests, friends assembling for a daytime outing or family members celebrating a special event gets everyone off to a great start.

We created a relaxed mood by serving breakfast at an island that doubles as the kitchen table. If your kitchen is small, you can have the meal in the dining room, family room or other comfortable space. Any breakfast calls for minimal fuss. After all, who wants to get up early to set a fancy table? We settled on simple potted flowers for decoration, complementing everyday dishware in a colorful floral pattern.

SINCE WEEKEND breakfasts tend to be more hearty, we chose to feature contemporary variations on rustic Italian favorites: polenta and sausage patties. Both dishes are also good served later in the day, should you change the occasion to a brunch. A classic sour cream coffee cake and papaya with raspberry-lime purée round out the menu.

Offer one or more fresh-squeezed juices to guests as well. We used the juice of blood oranges, available in well-stocked markets and good produce stores, as the basis for mimosas– a popular morning drink made of equal parts orange juice and Champagne or sparkling wine.

Menu

The bright floral pattern of everyday family china, including generously sized coffee mugs, establishes a festive tone. Vibrant red placemats boldly define each setting.

Beverage Ideas

Offer a choice of mimosas, juices and spiced coffees to your guests. Then, if you like, switch to a brut-style Champagne or sparkling wine. In addition, serve an off-dry white wine such as American Chenin Blanc, German Riesling or French Vouvray or a white Zinfandel or similar-styled blush wine with the meal.

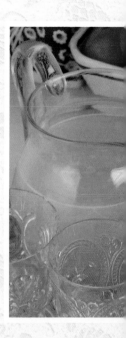

*Butternut Squash Polenta
with Greens & Fontina*

Turkey Sausage Patties

Sour Cream Coffee Cake

Papaya with Raspberry-Lime Purée

Small pots holding geraniums or primroses become cheerful centerpieces when wrapped or swagged with squares of colorful fabric (see page 188).

To coat glass rims with sugar for mimosas or juice, spread the sugar on a plate. Moisten the rims with a cut lemon and then dip in the sugar. Garnish each glass with organically grown edible flowers.

Preparation List

❧ The day before, bake the squash, make the polenta, shred the cheese and wash and sauté the greens. Assemble the sausage mixture and form into patties; make the raspberry-lime purée.

❧ The night before, bake the coffee cake.

❧ An hour before breakfast, peel and slice the papayas; assemble the ramekins or gratin dish for the polenta.

EACH RECIPE YIELDS 6 SERVINGS.

Butternut Squash Polenta with Greens & Fontina

SERVES 6

This blends a classic northern Italian ravioli filling and baked polenta. The greens provide a nice contrast between the sweetness of the squash and the richness of the cornmeal. The squash and polenta can be cooked 1 day in advance; the greens can be washed and cooked at the same time. An hour before, assemble the ramekins or gratin dish. For a simpler preparation to include with this menu, omit the greens and serve fried polenta with maple syrup (see below).

1 butternut squash, about 2½ lb (1.25 kg)
¼ cup (2 fl oz/60 ml) milk
¼ cup (2 oz/60 g) unsalted butter at
    room temperature
1 teaspoon freshly grated nutmeg, plus
    grated nutmeg to taste
pinch of ground cinnamon, optional
salt and freshly ground pepper
1½ cups (9 oz/235 g) medium-grind
    polenta or yellow cornmeal
5 cups (40 fl oz/1.25 l) water
⅔ cup (3 oz/90 g) freshly grated
    Parmesan cheese
2 tablespoons chopped fresh sage
2 tablespoons olive oil
1 yellow onion, diced
2 lb (1 kg) Swiss chard, kale or dande-
    lion greens, or a mixture, carefully
    washed and cut into strips
a few drops of balsamic vinegar or
    water
1 cup (4 oz/125 g) finely shredded
    Fontina cheese

Preheat an oven to 400°F (200°C). Place the squash in a baking pan and puncture with a knife in a few places. Bake until soft to the touch, about 1 hour. Remove from the oven and, when cool enough to handle, cut in half and scoop out the seeds and discard. Peel the squash and then mash the pulp in a bowl with a potato masher or fork, or pass it through a ricer into a bowl. Beat in the milk and butter until smooth. Season with the 1 teaspoon nutmeg, the cinnamon, if using, and salt and pepper to taste. Set aside.

🌱 Butter or line with parchment paper a 16-by-12-by-1-inch (40-by-30-by-2.5-cm) baking pan or a large, sided baking sheet.

🌱 In a large saucepan, combine the polenta and water. Bring to a boil over medium heat, stirring constantly. Reduce the heat to low and simmer uncovered, stirring often, until thickened and the polenta no longer tastes grainy. If the polenta is not yet cooked but is quite dry, add a little water.

🌱 When the polenta is ready, whisk in the squash mixture, Parmesan and sage until well mixed. Season to taste with salt, pepper and nutmeg. Pour into the prepared baking pan and refrigerate. When it has firmed up, cover well with plastic wrap and return to the refrigerator until very firm and well chilled.

🌱 In a large sauté pan or frying pan over medium heat, warm the olive oil. Add the onion and sauté until golden, about 15 minutes. Add the greens and sprinkle with the balsamic vinegar or water. Cook, stirring occasionally, until wilted and tender, about 8 minutes. Drain well and chop coarsely. Season to taste with salt and pepper.

🌱 Preheat an oven to 400°F (200°C). Butter six 4–6-inch (10–15-cm) individual ramekins or one 11-by-18-inch (28-by-46-cm) oval gratin dish.

🌱 Using a knife or biscuit cutter (for rounds), cut the polenta into desired shapes such as triangles, rectangles, rounds, squares or strips. Using a spatula, remove from the baking pan.

🌱 Layer half of the greens in the ramekins or gratin dish. Top with the polenta cutouts. (Reserve any leftover cutouts for another use.) Layer with the remaining greens; top with the Fontina.

🌱 Bake until heated through and the cheese is melted, about 20 minutes. Serve immediately.

Fried Polenta with Maple Syrup
Increase the ground cinnamon to 1 teaspoon and add the finely grated zest of 1 orange to the squash purée; omit the sage and the Parmesan. When the polenta is cold and firm, cut it into strips or triangles.

🌱 In a frying pan over medium-high heat, fry the polenta pieces in a few tablespoons of unsalted butter or olive oil until golden on both sides. Serve with maple syrup and with sautéed apple slices, if you like.

Butternut Squash Polenta
with Greens & Fontina

For guests who prefer tea with breakfast, offer full-flavored yet mild morning varieties such as Darjeeling, orange pekoe and English or Irish breakfast blends, along with herbal teas. If you use loose leaves instead of bags, tea infusers such as the one shown here—available in well-stocked kitchen stores and tea shops—brew individual cups in charming style.

Turkey Sausage Patties

SERVES 6

Here is a very lean sausage. You can increase the amount of nutmeg, allspice or mace for a more fragrant and sweeter taste. Adding the Calvados (an apple brandy), an orange-flavored liqueur and/or the orange zest deepens the flavor. You can make the sausage and form the patties 1 day ahead of serving.

2 lb (1 kg) ground (minced) turkey
2 teaspoons salt
2 teaspoons freshly ground pepper
2 teaspoons chopped fresh sage or
    ½ teaspoon dried sage
2 teaspoons chopped fresh thyme or
    ½ teaspoon dried thyme
½ teaspoon ground ginger
½ teaspoon ground nutmeg, allspice or
    mace
¼ cup (2 fl oz/60 ml) Calvados or
    orange-flavored liqueur, optional
2 teaspoons finely grated orange zest,
    optional (see page 185)
olive oil for frying

In a large bowl, combine the turkey, salt, pepper, sage, thyme, ginger and the nutmeg, allspice or mace, the Calvados or orange-flavored liqueur, if using, and the orange zest, if using. Mix together well. Scoop out a small nugget of the mixture, fry in a little olive oil, taste and adjust the seasonings.

🌲 Form the turkey mixture into 6–8 patties each about ½ inch (12 mm) thick.

🌲 In a large frying pan over high heat, warm a thin film of olive oil. Fry the patties, turning once, until golden and cooked through, about 4 minutes on each side. Serve immediately.

Butternut Squash Polenta with Greens & Fontina (page 109); Turkey Sausage Patties; Sour Cream Coffee Cake (page 112)

Sour Cream Coffee Cake

SERVES 6, WITH LEFTOVERS

Although this is not an unusual recipe for coffee cake, it is one of the very best you will find. The sour cream in the dough gives the cake a moist, rich texture. The traditional filling is made with pecans, but almonds or walnuts are equally suitable. If you like, add the raisins, dried currants, dates or apricots along with the nuts. A bundt pan or a tube pan works beautifully. The cake can be baked the night before, wrapped well and stored at room temperature.

Though coffee should be offered throughout the meal, it goes especially well with the cake. Be sure to brew only from freshly ground beans.

1 cup (4 oz/125 g) chopped pecans

1 tablespoon plus 2 cups (1 lb/500 g) sugar

1 teaspoon ground cinnamon

½ cup (3 oz/90 g) coarsely chopped raisins, apricots, pitted dates or whole dried currants, optional

2 cups (10 oz/315 g) all-purpose (plain) flour

1 teaspoon baking powder

¼ teaspoon salt

1 cup (8 oz/250 g) unsalted butter at room temperature

2 eggs

1 cup (8 fl oz/250 ml) sour cream

½ teaspoon vanilla extract (essence)

*P*reheat an oven to 350°F (180°C). Butter and flour a 9-inch (23-cm) tube or bundt pan. In a small bowl, stir together the pecans, the 1 tablespoon sugar, the cinnamon and the dried fruits, if using. Set aside.

🌳 In a bowl, sift together the flour, baking powder and salt. Set aside. In another bowl and using an electric mixer set on medium speed, beat together the butter and the remaining 2 cups (1 lb/500 g) sugar until light and fluffy. Beat in the eggs, one at a time, beating well after each addition. Reduce the speed to low and mix in the sour cream and vanilla. Then beat in the flour at low speed, one third at a time, just until incorporated. Spoon one third of the batter into the prepared pan. Sprinkle with the nut mixture. Spoon the remaining batter over the nut mixture, smoothing the top.

🌳 Bake until golden, about 1 hour. Let cool completely in the pan on a wire rack, then invert onto a serving plate.

Papaya with Raspberry-Lime Purée

SERVES 6

Easy and delicious, this is the ideal fruit accompaniment for this menu. The berry purée looks brilliant over the orange of the papaya. A few whole berries or thin strips of lime zest may be added as a garnish. The papaya can be peeled 2 hours before serving.

3 ripe papayas

3 cups (12 oz/375 g) raspberries

finely grated zest of 1 lime (see page 185)

2 tablespoons fresh lime juice

2 tablespoons sugar, or to taste

*P*eel the papayas, then cut in half lengthwise. Scoop out the seeds and discard. Cut lengthwise into slices ½ inch (12 mm) thick and arrange on individual plates.

🌳 In a food processor fitted with the metal blade or in a blender, purée the raspberries until smooth. Strain the purée through a fine-mesh sieve to remove any seeds and stir in the lime zest and juice and the sugar. Pour the raspberry purée over the papaya and serve at once.

Sour Cream Coffee Cake; Papaya with Raspberry-Lime Purée

FAMILY BIRTHDAY PARTY

A BIRTHDAY DINNER SHARED with family and close friends calls for a particularly light and cheerful mood. There's no need to dress up, to spend hours in the kitchen or to set an elaborate table. The party should instead focus on honoring the birthday celebrant.

We decided to hold our party late in the afternoon on a spring day, letting the bright sunshine add to the occasion's glow. But even if your guest of honor's day falls during the winter, an array of brightly colored tableware and linens, as well as centerpieces of complementary-colored flowers, peppers and lemons, can give the room a festive air just as surely as the more traditional balloons and streamers would. To set the table, we used more napkins as place mats, letting them hang slightly over the edge, instead of a tablecloth.

If you have a garden of blooming flowers, pick some to decorate the birthday table. Here, Icelandic poppies and anemones (both seasonally available from florists) form a colorful bouquet in a watering can before they are arranged.

Menu

NDIAN SPICES ENLIVEN the main course and side dishes in our birthday dinner menu. To leave you free to enjoy the celebration, most of the dishes are prepared ahead of the party day.

For such a close-knit gathering, we recommend serving most of the meal family style. The first-course soup might be ladled into bowls in the kitchen and carried out on a tray. The chicken, rice and vegetables follow on serving platters or in bowls, to be passed around the table. Dessert, however, calls for a special presentation: decorate a serving of profiteroles with a few brightly burning tapers for the celebrant to blow out.

Just inside the front door, an oversized basket with a handle holds birthday gifts that can be carried with ease to the honoree for opening.

Cold Cucumber Soup

Ginger & Orange Curried Fried Chicken

Mango Chutney

Saffron Rice

Corn with Chilies & Coconut Milk

Spinach with Peas & Mint

Almond Profiteroles with
Banana Ice Cream & Hot Fudge Sauce

A glazed earthenware plate reflects the bright, primary colors of the table linens and centerpieces. Napkins are informally rolled and secured with woven napkin rings.

Preparation List

❧ A few weeks before, make the chutney and store in the refrigerator.

❧ Two weeks before, make the fudge sauce.

❧ Two days before, mix the ice cream base.

❧ A day before, make the soup and the profiteroles; roast the chilies and wash the spinach. Freeze the ice cream.

❧ About two hours before, marinate the chicken and make the flour coating; prepare the corn base and soak the saffron rice. Shell and cook the peas.

EACH RECIPE YIELDS 6 SERVINGS.

Beverage Ideas

Champagne or sparkling wine is a must to celebrate the occasion. A light, red wine (Beaujolais, American Pinot Noir or Gamay) or a medium-bodied white (California Chardonnay, off-dry Riesling or Alsatian Gewürztraminer), or both, may accompany the food. For dessert, offer amaretto coffee or a Godiva chocolate liqueur.

Cold Cucumber Soup

SERVES 6

An ideal soup for a hot summer day. It can also be served hot instead of cold (see below). Mint, dill or basil is a refreshing and appropriate garnish to sprinkle on top. If you would like some added crunch, garnish each serving with chopped toasted walnuts, pine nuts or almonds. Prepare the soup the day before serving and chill well. Adjust seasoning at serving time.

2 tablespoons unsalted butter

1 yellow onion, diced

3–4 cups (24–32 fl oz/750 ml–1 l) chicken stock

1 small potato, about 4 oz (125 g), peeled and diced

3 cucumbers, peeled, seeded and diced

1 cup (8 oz/250 g) plain yogurt or ½ cup (4 fl oz/ 125 ml) heavy (double) cream

salt and freshly ground pepper

3 tablespoons chopped fresh dill, mint or basil

In a medium saucepan over medium heat, melt the butter. Add the onion and sauté until tender and translucent, about 10 minutes. Add 3 cups (24 fl oz/ 750 ml) of the chicken stock and the potato, raise the heat to high and bring to a boil. Reduce the heat to medium and simmer, uncovered, for 10 minutes. Add the cucumbers and continue to simmer until the cucumbers are soft, about 10 minutes longer.

🌳 Working in batches, transfer to a food processor fitted with the metal blade or to a blender and purée until smooth. If the purée is too thick, add as much of the remaining 1 cup (8 fl oz/ 250 ml) stock as needed to thin to a soup consistency. Transfer to a bowl, let cool slightly and then whisk in the yogurt or cream. Cover and refrigerate the soup until well chilled.

🌳 Add salt and pepper to taste and ladle into chilled bowls. Garnish with herb of choice and serve.

Hot Cucumber Soup

To serve the soup hot, omit the yogurt. Add ½ cup (4 fl oz/125 ml) sour cream or heavy (double) cream to the processor or blender and then purée the soup. Add the stock as needed to thin the purée and reheat gently. Season to taste with salt and pepper. Alternatively, omit the sour cream or heavy cream, reheat the purée and serve garnished with a dollop of plain yogurt.

These bright blue and green oversized bottles make creative decanters for wine.

Cold Cucumber Soup

Ginger & Orange Curried Fried Chicken

SERVES 6

Although frying the chicken must be done at the last minute, it marinates in the refrigerator for about 2 hours. Buttermilk and ginger tenderize the meat, so do not allow the chicken to stand in the marinade longer than the specified time. The curry-flavored flour can be mixed in a large paper bag or on a deep plate. You can also use bone-in chicken parts, but marinate them 3 hours and then fry, turning often, for 20–25 minutes. Offer 1 or 2 chicken breast halves per person.

2 cups (16 fl oz/500 ml) buttermilk

2 tablespoons grated, peeled fresh ginger (see page 185)

3 tablespoons grated orange zest (see page 185)

salt and freshly ground black pepper

12 half chicken breasts, boned, (5–6 oz/155–185 g each)

1½ cups (7½ oz/235 g) all-purpose (plain) flour

4–5 teaspoons curry powder

¾ teaspoon ground ginger

pinch cayenne pepper, optional

peanut oil for deep-frying

mango chutney (recipe on page 184) or high-quality bottled chutney

*I*n a shallow glass or plastic dish, combine the buttermilk, grated ginger, orange zest and salt and pepper to taste and mix well. Add the chicken, turning to coat well. Cover and marinate for 1–2 hours in the refrigerator.

🌳 In a large paper bag or on a deep plate, combine the flour, curry powder, ground ginger, salt and black pepper to taste and the cayenne pepper, if using.

🌳 Remove the chicken from the marinade and, a few pieces at a time, shake them in the bag of seasoned flour or coat them evenly in the seasoned flour on the plate.

🌳 In a large frying pan (or in 2 pans) over medium heat, pour in oil to a depth of 3 inches (7.5 cm) and heat to 375°F (190°C), or until a small cube of bread turns golden within moments of being dropped into it. When the oil is ready, add the chicken pieces and fry, turning once, until golden brown, 3–4 minutes on each side.

🌳 Using a slotted spatula, transfer to paper towels to drain briefly. Arrange on a warmed platter or individual plates and serve immediately with the chutney.

Saffron Rice

SERVES 6

Fragrant with whole spices, this golden yellow rice can be soaked about 2 hours before serving and then baked while you are frying the chicken, or it can also be baked in advance and then kept warm in the top pan of a double boiler or in a heatproof bowl placed over (but not touching) hot water. If you are not including fruits or nuts in other dishes in the meal, raisins or almonds are a good addition to the rice (see below).

2 cups (14 oz/440 g) basmati rice

6 qt (6 l) water

salt

¼ cup (2 fl oz/60 ml) dry white wine or water

1 teaspoon saffron threads

4–6 tablespoons (2–3 oz/60–90 g) unsalted butter

1 cinnamon stick, about 3 inches (5 cm) long

8 whole cloves

seeds from 8 cardamom pods

freshly ground pepper

*I*n a bowl combine the rice and water to cover by 1 inch (2.5 cm). Let stand for 2 hours; drain.

🌳 Preheat an oven to 350°F (180°C).

🌳 In a saucepan, bring the 6 qt (6 l) water to a boil and add salt to taste. Add the drained rice and boil for 10 minutes.

🌳 Drain the rice and rinse with warm water. Drain again and place in a shallow 1½-qt (1.5-l) baking dish measuring about 9 inches (23 cm) by 11 inches (28 cm) by 2 inches (5 cm).

🌳 Meanwhile, in a small pan over low heat, warm the wine or water; remove from the heat. Crush the saffron threads gently and add to the warm liquid. Let stand for 10 minutes.

🌳 In a small frying pan or saucepan over medium heat, melt the butter. Add the saffron and its soaking liquid, cinnamon, cloves, cardamom and pepper to taste and toss with the butter. Add the butter mixture to the rice, toss well and then cover the baking dish with aluminum foil.

🌳 Bake until the butter has been absorbed and the rice is tender but still firm, about 25 minutes. Remove the cinnamon stick and cloves and discard. Serve the rice hot.

Saffron Rice with Raisins or Almonds

Soak ½ cup (3 oz/90 g) raisins in hot water to cover until soft and plump, about 20 minutes. Drain and add to the butter with the spices. Or add ½ cup (3 oz/90 g) toasted almonds (see page 185) to the butter with the spices.

Ginger & Orange Curried Fried Chicken; Saffron Rice

Corn with Chilies & Coconut Milk

SERVES 6

Curried corn is incredibly sweet and aromatic. Summer white corn is best, but during the winter you may use frozen corn as well. You can also use corn stock in place of the chicken stock: combine the corn cobs with water to cover and boil for 30 minutes, then discard the cobs. The dish can be prepared up to the point where the coconut milk, stock and lemon zest are added 2 hours in advance and then finished just before serving.

1 teaspoon cumin seeds
2 tablespoons unsalted butter
¼ cup (¾ oz/20 g) minced green
   (spring) onions, including tender
   green tops
1 tablespoon ground coriander
⅛ teaspoon cayenne pepper
1 teaspoon curry powder
1 cup (8 fl oz/250 ml) coconut milk
½ cup (4 fl oz/125 ml) chicken stock
1 teaspoon finely grated lemon zest
   (see page 185)
4 cups (1½ lb/750 g) corn kernels
   (6–8 ears)
2 fresh pasilla chili peppers, roasted,
   peeled, deribbed and diced (see
   page 185)
4 tablespoons chopped fresh cilantro
   (fresh coriander)
salt and freshly ground black pepper

In a small, dry frying pan over medium heat, toast the cumin seeds, stirring or shaking the pan, until fragrant, about 3 minutes. Transfer to a spice grinder or a mortar and finely grind; set aside.

In a large saucepan over medium heat, melt the butter. Add the green onions and sauté, stirring, until tender, about 5 minutes. Stir in the coriander, cumin, cayenne and curry powder and sauté for 3 minutes longer.

Add the coconut milk, stock and lemon zest and bring to a simmer, stirring to mix well. Add the corn and continue to simmer until the corn is almost tender, about 3 minutes.

Fold in the chilies and the cilantro and cook for 1 minute longer. Season to taste with salt and pepper.

Transfer to a serving dish and serve at once.

Spinach with Peas & Mint

SERVES 6

This leafy curry is a fine foil for the richness of the chicken and the sweetness of the corn. Swiss chard (silverbeet) can be used in place of the spinach. The greens can be washed and dried up to a day ahead and stored in the crisper section of the refrigerator; shell and cook the peas up to 2 hours in advance. Thawed frozen peas can be substituted for the cooked fresh peas.

1 teaspoon fennel seeds
1 teaspoon cumin seeds
¼ cup (2 oz/60 g) unsalted butter or
   (2 fl oz/60 ml) olive oil
1 tablespoon grated, peeled fresh ginger
   (see page 185)
¼ teaspoon ground cloves
3 lb (1.5 kg) spinach, carefully washed,
   stems removed and cut into strips
   ½ inch (12 mm) wide
2 teaspoons finely grated lemon zest
   (see page 185)
1 cup (5 oz/155 g) shelled green peas
   (about 1 lb/500 g unshelled), cooked
   in boiling water until tender-crisp,
   2–5 minutes, and drained
salt and freshly ground pepper
½ cup (¾ oz/20 g) chopped fresh mint

In a small, dry frying pan over medium heat, toast the fennel and cumin seeds, stirring or shaking the pan, until fragrant, about 3 minutes. Transfer to a spice grinder or a mortar and finely grind; set aside.

In a large, wide sauté pan over medium heat, melt the butter or warm the olive oil. Add the ground fennel and cumin, ginger and cloves and stir until heated through. Add the spinach and stir and toss until wilted, 3–5 minutes, adding a bit of water if the spinach begins to scorch.

Stir in the lemon zest and peas and heat through. Season to taste with salt and pepper.

Add the mint, toss well and transfer to a serving dish. Serve immediately.

Corn with Chilies & Coconut Milk;
Spinach with Peas & Mint

Almond Profiteroles with Banana Ice Cream & Hot Fudge Sauce

SERVES 6

Instead of a birthday cake, why not surprise everyone with these mini–cream puffs filled with banana ice cream and topped with a thick, rich hot fudge sauce. Put a candle on the birthday celebrant's portion and enjoy the party. The profiteroles can be prepared the day before, stored in a covered metal container and then warmed in a 350°F (180°C) oven for 5 minutes to recrisp them. The fudge sauce can be made up to 2 weeks in advance, refrigerated and then gently reheated. The ice cream base can be made 2 days in advance and then frozen the day before serving. Since bananas quickly darken after peeling, don't puree them until the moment you are ready to mix the bananas into the ice cream base.

FOR THE ICE CREAM:

6 egg yolks
2 cups (16 fl oz/500 ml) milk
2 cups (16 fl oz/500 ml) heavy (double) cream
¾ cup (6 oz/185 g) sugar
½ teaspoon freshly grated nutmeg
1 cup (8 oz/250 g) puréed ripe bananas (about 2 bananas)
1 teaspoon vanilla extract (essence)
¼ teaspoon salt

FOR THE PROFITEROLES:

1 cup (8 fl oz/250 ml) water
¼ teaspoon salt
½ cup (4 oz/125 g) unsalted butter, cut into pieces
1 cup (5 oz/155 g) all-purpose (plain) flour
1 tablespoon sugar
5 eggs
½ cup (2½ oz/75 g) chopped toasted almonds (see page 185)

hot fudge sauce (recipe on page 184)

To make the ice cream, place the egg yolks in a bowl and beat lightly with a fork until blended.

In a saucepan over medium heat, combine the milk, cream, sugar and nutmeg. Heat, stirring to dissolve the sugar, until small bubbles form along the edge of the pan. Stir in the bananas. Gradually add a little of the hot cream mixture to the yolks, whisking constantly. Whisk in a bit more of the cream mixture, then whisk the yolk mixture into the hot cream mixture. Cook over medium heat, stirring constantly, until the custard coats the back of a spoon, 3–5 minutes.

Strain the custard through a fine-mesh sieve into a bowl and then nest in an ice bath. Stir in the vanilla and salt. When cool, remove from the ice bath, cover and refrigerate overnight to develop the flavors.

The next day, taste and adjust the sweetness and amount of vanilla or nutmeg, as necessary. Pour into an ice cream maker and freeze according to the manufacturer's instructions.

To make the profiteroles, preheat an oven to 375°F (190°C). In a saucepan, combine the water, salt and butter and bring slowly to a boil. Remove from the heat and add the flour and sugar all at once. Return the pan to medium heat and cook, stirring vigorously, until the mixture forms a dry ball and pulls away from the sides of the pan, about 4 minutes.

Remove from the heat and transfer the dough to a bowl. Then, using an electric mixer set on medium speed, beat in the eggs, one at a time, beating well after each addition. When all the eggs have been added, the mixture should be smooth and glossy and stiff enough to hold its shape. Spoon the profiterole pastry onto ungreased baking sheets, forming mounds about 1 inch (2.5 cm) in diameter for small profiteroles or 1½–2 inches (4–5 cm) in diameter for medium-sized profiteroles. You should have 18 small or 12 medium pastries in all. Sprinkle with the almonds.

Bake until golden brown, about 20 minutes. Turn off the oven. Make 1 or 2 tiny slits in the side of each profiterole to let the steam escape. Position the oven door slightly ajar and leave the puffs in the oven to cool and dry, about 20 minutes.

To serve, split the pastries in half and arrange on individual plates. Fill the bottom halves with the banana ice cream and replace the tops. Spoon the hot fudge sauce over the tops and serve immediately.

Almond Profiteroles with Banana Ice Cream & Hot Fudge Sauce

BACKYARD BARBECUE

THE WARMEST, MOST leisurely time of the year lures us outdoors to entertain, whether we are celebrating a public holiday, a family anniversary or nothing at all. The meal itself, cooked in the open air, becomes the occasion.

We set our early evening party in a large garden with a built-in stone barbecue. But, you could hold it on any patio large enough for an outdoor grill or even in an apartment, with the food cooked on a small barbecue on the balcony or in the kitchen broiler (griller). Oversized, brightly colored dishware, in this case Provençal pottery, holds generous servings and emphasizes the sunny spirit of the season, as do blossoms gathered from the garden or bought from the florist and, if space allows, pots and urns of live seasonal flowers.

EVERAL SUN-DRENCHED cuisines contribute to our backyard barbecue menu. India, where foods are often cooked in a tandoor oven, inspired the appetizer. A Middle Eastern marinade flavors the pork loin, and Southwestern corn and Mediterranean tomato salads round out the offerings. The only cooking to do during the party itself is grilling the shrimp and pork, both quick, simple tasks. All recipes double or triple easily if the guest list grows.

The menu is meant to be served buffet style, so have dishes and platters on hand, with plates, napkins and cutlery stacked nearby. If you have picnic baskets or hampers, you might use them to carry all the serving pieces outside, and then leave them in view to underscore the ambience of an at-home picnic. Provide guests with seating at tables, on benches, or should they succumb fully to summer's allure, on blankets or cushions on the grassy lawn.

Menu

Beverage Ideas

Wine spritzers or a zesty summer punch make a good start. Follow with an assortment of medium-bodied beers, red wines such as Zinfandel, Beaujolais or Italian Dolcetto and fragrant whites: Chardonnay, Chenin Blanc or a white Rhône.

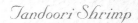

Tandoori Shrimp

*Pork Loin with
Pomegranate & Orange Glaze*

Apricot Mustard

Cheddar Chive Biscuits

*Tomato Salad with
Basil-Honey Vinaigrette*

Corn Salad

Peach Bread Pudding

Summer flowers and foliage are gathered from the garden for decorations. Proper gloves, clippers and a basket ease the work.

Preparation List

❧ You can make the apricot mustard two to three weeks (or up to several months) before.

❧ If serving the raspberry-lime purée with the bread pudding, make it the day before.

❧ The night before, marinate the pork and prepare the tandoori marinade.

❧ Make the corn salad, the bread pudding and the vinaigrette six hours before.

❧ Two hours before, slice the tomatoes.

❧ An hour before, marinate the shrimp, make the fire and form the biscuits.

EACH RECIPE YIELDS 6 SERVINGS.

Guests can help themselves to chilled white wine in wicker-insulated carafes or a selection of beers on ice in any lined container. Arrange good-sized glasses nearby and don't forget the bottle opener.

Tandoori Shrimp

SERVES 6

Shrimp is always popular, but if your budget is tight, cubes of fish or boneless chicken breast meat can be substituted (see below). The marinade can be made the night before, but be sure to marinate the shrimp only 1–2 hours. The shrimp can also be skewered and cooked in a preheated broiler (griller), or they can be sautéed in unsalted butter or peanut or olive oil. Soak the skewers while the charcoal heats in the grill.

2 cloves garlic, minced

1 piece fresh ginger, about 2 inches (5 cm) long, peeled and cut up

3 tablespoons fresh lemon or lime juice

¼ teaspoon ground turmeric

1 tablespoon ground cumin

½ teaspoon salt

2 fresh jalapeño (hot green) chili peppers, seeded, if desired, and minced

1 cup (8 oz/250 g) nonfat plain yogurt

1 tablespoon paprika, plus paprika for garnish

1½ lb (750 g) large shrimp (prawns), peeled and deveined

lemon or lime wedges

In a food processor fitted with the metal blade or in a blender, combine the garlic, ginger, lemon or lime juice, turmeric, cumin, salt, jalapeños, yogurt and the 1 tablespoon paprika. Process until well blended. Transfer to a glass or plastic bowl, add the shrimp and toss to coat evenly. Cover and marinate in the refrigerator for about 1 hour.

Place 12 bamboo skewers in water to cover to soak for 15–30 minutes. Prepare a fire in a charcoal grill.

Drain the skewers, then remove the shrimp from the marinade. Holding 2 skewers parallel, thread 4 or 5 of the shrimp onto the pair of skewers, holding the shrimp flat. (Parallel skewers make turning the shrimp on the grill easier.) Repeat with the remaining shrimp and skewers. Place on an oiled grill rack and grill for 2 minutes. Turn the shrimp and grill until the shrimp turn pink, about 2 minutes longer.

Sprinkle with paprika and serve immediately with lemon or lime wedges.

Fish or Chicken Tandoori

If using fish, substitute any firm white fish fillets, such as bass, swordfish or flounder, for the shrimp. Cut into 1½-inch (4-cm) cubes, marinate for no longer than 1–2 hours and thread onto single rather than parallel skewers. Grill as directed for the shrimp, cooking until opaque at the center. If using chicken, cut chicken breast meat into 1½-inch (4-cm) cubes for skewering. Marinate for as long as 4–5 hours and then thread onto single skewers. Grill as directed for shrimp, cooking until opaque at the center.

Tandoori Shrimp

Pork Loin with Pomegranate & Orange Glaze

SERVES 6

Pomegranate syrup is available in specialty markets. Fresh or bottled pomegranate juice can be reduced over high heat to a syrupy consistency. Marinate the pork in the spice paste overnight for fullest flavor. The tenderloins can also be cooked in a broiler (griller) or the loin can be roasted in the oven (see right).

1 boneless pork loin, about 3 lb (1.5 kg), tied for roasting, or 3 pork tenderloins, about 1 lb (500 g) each

FOR THE SPICE PASTE:

2 teaspoons minced garlic
2 tablespoons apricot mustard (see page 133) or hot Dijon mustard
finely grated zest of 1 orange (see page 185)
⅓ cup (3 fl oz/80 ml) fresh orange juice
2 tablespoons grated, peeled fresh ginger
2 tablespoons pomegranate syrup
2 tablespoons soy sauce

FOR THE BASTING SAUCE:

⅓ cup (3 fl oz/80 ml) fresh orange juice
3 tablespoons honey
3 tablespoons pomegranate syrup
2 tablespoons soy sauce

𝒫lace the pork in a glass or plastic dish. To make the spice paste, in a bowl, combine the garlic, mustard, orange zest and juice, ginger, pomegranate syrup and soy sauce. Rub onto the meat, cover and marinate for at least 6 hours or overnight in the refrigerator. Bring to room temperature before grilling.

🌳 Prepare a fire in a charcoal grill.

🌳 To make the basting sauce, in a small bowl, mix the orange juice, honey, pomegranate syrup and soy sauce.

🌳 Place the pork loin or tenderloins on an oiled grill rack not too close to the heat source. Grill, brushing with the basting sauce and turning often until nicely glazed, 15–20 minutes on each

Pork Loin with Pomegranate & Orange Glaze; Apricot Mustard; Cheddar Chive Biscuits

side for the large loin and 5 minutes per side for the smaller tenderloins, or until an instant-read meat thermometer registers 140°F (60°C) for medium.

🌳 Transfer the pork to a work surface, cover with an aluminum foil tent and let rest for 8–10 minutes. Snip the strings if tied and thinly slice across the grain. Serve at once.

Roast Pork Loin

To roast the pork loin in the oven, preheat the oven to 400°F (200°C). You will need to make only half a recipe of the basting sauce. Place the marinated pork loin in a roasting pan and roast, brushing often with the basting sauce, until nicely glazed, about 1 hour and 10 minutes or until an instant-read meat thermometer registers 140°F (60°C) for medium.

Apricot Mustard

MAKES ABOUT 3 CUPS (1½ LB/750 G)

This mustard must be made 2–3 weeks in advance of serving to allow the flavors to mellow. It can be stored in the refrigerator for up to several months. Or, ladle it into hot, sterilized jars and process for 10 minutes (see Canning Preserves, page 185), in which case it can be stored for 6 months.

1 cup (3 oz/90 g) dry mustard
½ cup (4 fl oz/125 ml) cider vinegar
6 oz (185 g) dried apricots
1 cup (8 fl oz/250 ml) hot water, or to cover
½ cup (4 fl oz/125 ml) orange juice, or as needed
1 cup (7 oz/220 g) firmly packed dark brown sugar
½ teaspoon salt
½ teaspoon ground cinnamon
¼ teaspoon ground ginger

In a bowl, whisk together the dry mustard and vinegar. Let stand for 1 hour. Meanwhile, in a small saucepan, combine the apricots and the water. Let stand for 30 minutes.

🌳 Place the pan with the apricots over medium heat, bring to a simmer and simmer, uncovered, for 5 minutes to soften. Remove from the heat.

🌳 In a food processor fitted with the metal blade, combine the apricots and any liquid remaining in the pan and the orange juice and purée until smooth. Add the mustard-vinegar mixture, brown sugar, salt, cinnamon and ginger and process to mix well.

🌳 Transfer to a container, cover tightly and refrigerate.

An assortment of colorful cotton throws, pillows and straw hats invites guests to relax. Keep a good supply of sunscreen on hand, too.

Cheddar Chive Biscuits

MAKES 1 DOZEN

A nice variation on the basic biscuit. These are a fine foil for the richness of the pork. The biscuits can be cut out and arranged on a baking sheet 1 hour before baking.

2 cups (10 oz/315 g) all-purpose (plain) flour
1 tablespoon baking powder
1 teaspoon baking soda (sodium bicarbonate)
1 teaspoon salt
1 teaspoon sugar
½ cup (4 oz/125 g) unsalted butter, chilled
4 tablespoons minced fresh chives
1 cup (8 fl oz/250 ml) buttermilk
½ cup (2 oz/60 g) coarsely shredded Cheddar cheese

*Pre*heat an oven to 400°F (200°C).

🌳 In a bowl, stir together the flour, baking powder, baking soda, salt and sugar. Using a pastry blender or 2 table knives, cut in the butter until the mixture resembles cornmeal. Make a well in the center of the mixture.

🌳 In a small bowl, stir the chives into the buttermilk. Pour the buttermilk into the well and add the cheese. Stir quickly to combine, just until the dough pulls away from the sides of the bowl, 1–2 minutes. Turn out onto a floured work surface and knead gently and quickly until the dough is no longer sticky, 3 or 4 turns. Pat into a square ½ inch (12 mm) thick. Dip a 2½ inches (6 cm) in diameter or square biscuit cutter or glass in flour, then cut out 12 round or square biscuits.

🌳 Place biscuits on an ungreased baking sheet and bake until pale gold, 12–15 minutes. Serve hot.

Tomato Salad with Basil-Honey Vinaigrette

SERVES 6

This aromatic dressing also complements avocados and pears or melon. Some balsamic vinegars are sharper than others, so start with 3 tablespoons and add more as needed to taste. Do not use strong olive oil for this recipe or the balance of sweet and sour will be overwhelmed. If you cannot find beefsteak tomatoes, any ripe, fresh variety will do. The vinaigrette can be made 6 hours in advance and the tomatoes can be sliced 2 hours in advance, but do not drizzle the vinaigrette over the tomatoes until just before serving.

FOR THE VINAIGRETTE:

3–4 tablespoons balsamic vinegar
3 tablespoons full-flavored honey
1 teaspoon salt
¾ cup (6 fl oz/180 ml) mild olive oil
½ cup (¾ oz/20 g) tightly packed
   chopped fresh basil

2–2½ lb (1–1.25 kg) ripe beefsteak or
   other flavorful tomatoes

To make the vinaigrette, in a small bowl, whisk together the vinegar, honey and salt. Add the olive oil and basil and whisk to blend well. Taste and adjust the seasonings.

🌳 Slice the tomatoes and arrange on a platter. Drizzle the vinaigrette over the tomatoes and serve.

*Tomato Salad with
Basil-Honey Vinaigrette*

Corn Salad

SERVES 6

This salad says summer. Of course, just-picked sweet corn can make a difference. The tomatoes can be peeled, if you like. The salad will hold for up to 6 hours and is best served at room temperature.

6 ears corn
½ cup (4 fl oz/125 ml) olive oil
1 cup (5 oz/155 g) minced red
    (Spanish) onion
2 teaspoons chili powder
1 teaspoon ground cumin
1 red bell pepper (capsicum), seeded,
    deribbed and cut into ¼-inch
    (6-mm) dice
1 green bell pepper (capsicum), seeded,
    deribbed and cut into ¼-inch
    (6-mm) dice
1–1½ cups (6–9 oz/185–280 g) seeded
    and diced tomatoes
4 tablespoons chopped fresh cilantro
    (fresh coriander)
3 tablespoons sherry vinegar, or to taste
salt and freshly ground pepper

Shuck corn and rub off the silk. Using a sharp knife, hold each ear of corn firmly and cut off the kernels. You should have approximately 3 cups (18 oz/560 g) of kernels.

🌳 Bring a saucepan three-fourths full of salted water to a boil. Add the corn kernels and boil for 1–2 minutes. Drain and immerse in cold water to stop the cooking. Drain again and pat dry with paper towels.

🌳 In a small sauté pan over medium heat, warm ¼ cup (2 fl oz/60 ml) of the olive oil. Add the onion and sauté for a few minutes, just to take the sharp bite out. Add the chili powder and cumin and sauté for 1 minute longer.

🌳 In a serving bowl, combine the corn, red and green bell peppers, tomatoes and cooled onions. Toss to mix. Add the cilantro, the remaining ¼ cup (2 fl oz/60 ml) olive oil and the vinegar. Toss well to combine. Season to taste with salt and pepper, toss again and serve.

Corn Salad

Peach Bread Pudding

SERVES 6

The lime-scented raspberry purée is a particularly nice touch but not absolutely necessary for this old-fashioned dessert. All you truly need for this delicate summer pudding are flavorful ripe peaches. The almond-scented amaretto liqueur gives the peaches a pleasing fragrance and flavor. The pudding can be baked up to 6 hours before serving. If you are serving the raspberry purée as well, it can be made 1 day ahead. Be sure to have a kettle or saucepan full of hot water on hand while assembling.

6 tablespoons (3 oz/90 g) unsalted butter, melted and clarified

12 slices fine-textured white bread or brioche, cut into 1-inch (2.5-cm) cubes

4 cups (32 fl oz/1 l) heavy (double) cream

6 large ripe peaches, peeled, pitted and cut into ¾-inch (2-cm) cubes

¼ cup (2 fl oz/60 ml) amaretto liqueur

4 whole eggs, plus 4 egg yolks

¾ cup (6 oz/185 g) sugar

1 teaspoon vanilla extract (essence)

½ teaspoon almond extract (essence)

raspberry-lime purée (recipe on page 112), optional

Preheat an oven to 300°F (150°C).

☘ In a large frying pan over medium-high heat, warm 3 tablespoons of the butter. Add half of the bread cubes and fry, stirring, until golden on all sides, 3–4 minutes. Using a slotted spoon, transfer to paper towels to drain. Repeat with 3 more tablespoons butter and the remaining bread cubes.

☘ In a saucepan over medium heat, warm the cream until small bubbles appear at the edge of the pan. Meanwhile, in a bowl, combine the peaches and amaretto and toss to mix.

☘ In another bowl, combine the whole eggs, egg yolks and sugar and, using a whisk, beat until frothy.

☘ Whisk about ½ cup (4 fl oz/125 ml) of the hot cream into the egg mixture, then gradually whisk in the remaining cream. Stir in the vanilla and almond extracts. To remove any lumps, pour the mixture through a fine-mesh sieve into a clean pitcher or bowl.

☘ Combine the peaches and bread cubes in a 3-qt (3-l) shallow rectangular or oval baking dish. Mix to distribute evenly. Slowly pour in the custard, being careful not to disturb the peach mixture. Place the baking dish in a large roasting pan and pour hot water into the pan to reach halfway up the sides of the dish. Bake until the custard is just set, about 1½ hours; it should still be slightly wobbly in the center.

☘ Let cool on a wire rack. Serve with the raspberry-lime purée, if desired.

Peach Bread Pudding

BRUNCH FOR HOUSEGUESTS

WHEN FRIENDS OR family are visiting for the weekend, Sunday brunch is commonly the one at-home meal shared by everyone. Stretching in leisurely fashion from late morning to early afternoon, brunch ranks among the most popular types of get-togethers. With a little planning, it can also be among the easiest to organize and prepare, keeping you out of the kitchen and enjoying the company.

We suggest setting the table the night before or as soon as possible after you wake up, while your houseguests are pouring their first cups of coffee or tea. If the weather is nice and your home allows, choose an outdoor setting such as a patio or deck. Otherwise, pick the most comfortable spot available, plumping cushions on cozy chairs for everyone to sit on and relax.

Purchased at a local nursery, small cacti are displayed in terra-cotta, stone and frosted-glass containers. They make charming table centerpieces as well as permanent patio or sunroom additions.

Menu

A lively selection of authentic Mexican specialties, this brunch menu features eggs, sausage and seafood that perfectly bridge breakfast and lunch. Inspired by the food's bright colors and flavors, we accessorized the meal using a striped tablecloth that recalls native blankets and bandannas as napkins.

Bloody Marys with a spicy south-of-the-border twist pique appetites while you do the final cooking. Mexican-style hot chocolate, spiced coffee and sugar-coated cookies draw out the meal's conclusion, encouraging guests to linger over the Sunday papers or lose themselves in conversation.

Shown here on a rustic bench on the patio, the menu's colorful fruits and vegetables may also be used as impromptu decorations for a daytime party.

Spicy Bloody Marys

Scallop Seviche with Grapefruit

Huevos Rancheros, Yucatecan Style

Chorizo Patties

Mexican Wedding Cookies

Mexican Hot Chocolate or Mexican Coffee

Preparation List

❧ Soak the black beans two nights before and then cook them the next day.

❧ Bake the cookies a couple of days before.

❧ The day before, make the chorizo mixture and the spicy tomato sauce.

❧ Three to four hours before, combine the scallops and citrus juices for the seviche.

❧ Just before serving, add the grapefruit and avocado to the seviche.

EACH RECIPE YIELDS 6 SERVINGS, EXCEPT BLOODY MARY RECIPE.

Beverage Ideas

A spicy Bloody Mary or fresh-squeezed citrus juice will start everyone off on the right foot. Stay with these drinks or move on to medium-bodied Mexican beers or a spicy red wine such as Côtes du Rhône, a light Zinfandel or a Shiraz. Cap off the morning with the flavors of Mexico, serving either Mexican hot chocolate or coffee.

The cool blue-and-white motifs of the tablecloth, dishes and napkins complement the hot colors and spicy flavors of the menu.

Spicy Bloody Mary

SERVES 1

Here's a Latin American twist on the classic Bloody Mary. The Worcestershire sauce usually added to this brunch favorite has been omitted because it does not mix well with tequila.

¼ teaspoon minced fresh jalapeño (hot green)chili pepper
3 fl oz (90 ml) tomato juice
1½ fl oz (45 ml) tequila or pepper vodka
1 tablespoon fresh lemon juice
4 or 5 drops hot-pepper sauce, such as Tabasco
salt and freshly ground pepper
ice cubes

For an extra-spicy drink, combine the jalapeño and tomato juice in a glass and let stand for 15–20 minutes. Then combine the tomato juice, tequila or vodka, lemon juice, hot-pepper sauce and salt and pepper to taste in a cocktail shaker and shake vigorously. Strain into a tall glass filled with ice cubes and serve.

Scallop Seviche with Grapefruit

SERVES 6

Here is a refreshing seafood, grapefruit and avocado first course that is best for a brunch that starts in the late morning or at noon because it must be made at least 3 hours but no more than 4 hours before serving. While the small bay scallops are best, sea scallops will also work. Cut them horizontally if they are very thick, and then cut them in half if they are wide as well. If you cannot find small grapefruits, cut the sections of larger grapefruits in half so they are bite-sized. You can use either white or pink grapefruit or, as we did, a mixture of both. You can also make this with shrimp (prawns) or a firm white fish (see below).

1½ lb (750 g) bay scallops
⅔ cup (5 fl oz/160 ml) fresh lime juice
⅔ cup (5 fl oz/160 ml) fresh grapefruit juice
1 red (Spanish) onion, finely diced
2 fresh jalapeño (hot green) chili peppers, seeded, if desired, and minced

1 teaspoon salt, or to taste
¼ cup (2 fl oz/60 ml) olive oil
3 tablespoons minced fresh cilantro (fresh coriander)
1 teaspoon grated, peeled fresh ginger (optional)
1 red bell pepper (capsicum), seeded, deribbed and finely diced (optional)
3 small grapefruits, peeled, with all white membrane removed, and sectioned
2 large avocados, halved, pitted, peeled and diced

Place the scallops in a glass or plastic dish. Pour on the lime and grapefruit juices. Turn the scallops over to coat them well, then cover and refrigerate for 2–3 hours.

🌳 Add the onion, jalapeños, salt, olive oil, cilantro and the ginger and bell pepper, if using. Cover and refrigerate for 1 hour longer. Toss in the grapefruits and avocados and transfer to a serving dish. Serve immediately.

Seviche with Other Seafood

To make a shrimp seviche, peel and devein 1½ lb (750 g) shrimp (prawns) and cut in half lengthwise. Proceed as directed above for scallops. To make white fish seviche, cut 1½ lb (750 g) firm white fish fillets such as snapper, rock cod or halibut into pieces 1½ inches (4 cm) long by ¼ inch (6 mm) wide. Proceed as directed above for scallops.

Offer Bloody Mary fixings (leave out the alcohol for a Virgin Mary) on a separate table. For pepper vodka, steep 4 small hot chili peppers in a bottle of vodka for 7 to 10 days.

Spicy Bloody Mary; Scallop Seviche with Grapefruit

Huevos Rancheros, Yucatecan Style; Chorizo Patties

Huevos Rancheros, Yucatecan Style

SERVES 6

In the Yucatán, cooks top the sauce with a few blanched peas and some diced cooked ham. If you omit the chorizo patties, include the peas and ham garnish here. If you cannot find flavorful tomatoes, use 3 cups (18 oz/560 g) canned plum (Roma) tomatoes, with their juices, and omit the broiling. The beans can be started 2 nights ahead and chilled. The sauce can be made 1 day in advance. Before serving, mash and fry the beans, warm the tortillas and fry the eggs.

FOR THE BLACK BEANS:

1½ cups (10½ oz/330 g) dried black beans

8 cups (64 fl oz/2 l) water

2 cloves garlic

1 small yellow onion, diced

1 small piece cinnamon stick

salt

FOR THE SPICY TOMATO SAUCE:

2 lb (1 kg) vine-ripened tomatoes

1 fresh jalapeño (hot green) chili pepper, seeded, if desired, and coarsely chopped

½ yellow onion, cut up

1 clove garlic, cut up

1 tablespoon olive oil

salt and freshly ground pepper

½ cup (4 fl oz/125 ml) fresh orange juice, optional

FOR THE FINISHED DISH:

2 tablespoons olive oil or lard

1 small yellow onion, minced

1 clove garlic, minced

6 corn tortillas

vegetable or olive oil, for warming tortillas and frying eggs

12 eggs

½ cup (2½ oz/75 g) crumbled mild feta, fresh goat cheese or other mild fresh cheese, optional

To prepare the beans, pick over and discard any stones or misshapen beans. Place the beans in a bowl and add water to cover generously. Cover and refrigerate overnight. Drain well. Transfer the beans to a saucepan, add the water and bring to a boil. Add the garlic, onion and cinnamon stick, cover, reduce the heat to medium-low and simmer until tender, about 1 hour, adding salt to taste midway through cooking.

❧ Remove from the heat, then remove the cinnamon stick and discard. Taste and adjust the salt. Do not drain. Set aside or refrigerate until needed (up to 1 day).

❧ To make the tomato sauce, preheat a broiler (griller). Line a baking sheet with aluminum foil and place the tomatoes on it. Place in the broiler and broil (grill), turning occasionally, until soft and blackened on all sides, 4–6 minutes. Remove from the broiler and, when cool enough to handle, peel and chop them, capturing any juices that are released.

❧ In a food processor fitted with the metal blade or in a blender, combine the tomatoes, jalapeño, onion and garlic and purée until smooth. In a saucepan, over medium-high heat, warm the 1 tablespoon of olive oil. When it is quite hot, add the tomato purée; it will bubble up, so be careful to avoid splashes. Continue to simmer over low heat, adding a little water if it dries out, about 5 minutes. Season to taste with salt and pepper. For a Yucatecan accent, stir in the orange juice; set aside.

❧ To finish the dish, in a large sauté pan over medium heat, warm the 2 tablespoons of olive oil or melt the lard. Add the onion and garlic and sauté until tender and translucent, about 8 minutes. Add half of the beans and a little of their liquid and, using a potato masher or a large fork, mash the beans. Add the remaining beans and as much of their liquid as necessary to achieve a good consistency and again mash the beans. They should remain a little chunky. Cook, stirring, until warmed through. Cover and keep warm over low heat.

❧ Reheat the sauce to serving temperature. Cover and keep warm.

❧ To soften the tortillas, heat a large frying pan or a griddle over medium heat. Add enough oil to form a film. Add the tortillas, one at a time, and heat, turning once, until warmed and pliable, about 1 minute on each side. Transfer to a large sheet of aluminum foil, then wrap tightly to keep warm.

❧ In the same pan (or in 2 pans) over medium heat, again add enough oil to form a film. Working in batches if necessary, fry the eggs, sunny side up, to desired doneness. Remove from the heat.

❧ Divide the tortillas among 6 warmed plates. Spread an equal amount of beans on each tortilla, then top each serving with 2 eggs. Drizzle the tomato sauce over the eggs and garnish with the cheese, if using. Serve immediately.

Generous drinks and chairs comfortably outfitted with cushions encourage guests to while away the morning.

Chorizo Patties

SERVES 6

Purchase pork that is not too lean for the best results. The chorizo mixture can be assembled and chilled a day ahead. Cook the patties just before you fry the beans and eggs and keep them warm in a 350°F (180°C) oven.

2 lb (1 kg) ground (minced) pork, well chilled

¼ lb (125 g) fatback, finely chopped or coarsely ground, well chilled (about ⅔ cup)

8–10 cloves garlic, minced

1 tablespoon ground oregano

1 teaspoon ground cinnamon

1 teaspoon freshly ground black pepper

¼ teaspoon ground cloves

1 tablespoon salt

1–2 teaspoons cayenne pepper

¼ cup (1½ oz/45 g) paprika

½ cup (4 fl oz/125 ml) red wine vinegar or sherry vinegar

olive or vegetable oil for frying

Thoroughly combine the pork, fatback, garlic, oregano, cinnamon, black pepper, cloves, salt, cayenne pepper, paprika and vinegar in a chilled bowl. In a large, lightly oiled sauté pan or griddle over medium heat, sauté a spoonful of the mixture until cooked. Taste and adjust the seasonings. Form the mixture into 6 patties about ½ inch (12 mm) thick.

❧ In the same pan or griddle, add enough oil to form a film. Sauté the patties, turning them once, until golden brown and cooked through, about 4 minutes on each side. Or, preheat a broiler (griller) and place the patties on a broiler pan. Broil (grill), turning once, until golden brown and cooked through, 3–4 minutes on each side. Serve immediately or keep warm in a preheated oven.

Mexican Wedding Cookies

MAKES ABOUT 3 DOZEN

There is no need to wait for a wedding to make these cookies. They are an ideal accompaniment to Mexican coffee. They can be baked 2 days ahead and stored in an airtight container at room temperature. If they will not all be eaten at brunch, roll in confectioners' sugar only as many as you think will be eaten; uncoated cookies can be kept in an airtight tin for up to 1 week. Dust with sugar just before serving.

1 cup (8 oz/250 g) unsalted butter at
    room temperature
⅓ cup (3 oz/90 g) granulated sugar
1 teaspoon vanilla extract (essence)
finely grated zest of 2 oranges (see
    page 185)
¼ cup (2 fl oz/60 ml) fresh orange juice
2 egg yolks
3 cups (15 oz/470 g) all-purpose
    (plain) flour
1 cup (4 oz/125 g) pecans, toasted and
    finely ground (see page 185)
1 cup (4 oz/125 g) confectioners'
    (icing) sugar

In a large bowl, combine the butter and granulated sugar. Using an electric mixer set on medium speed, beat the mixture, scraping down the sides of the bowl occasionally, until it is fluffy and light, about 5–8 minutes. Add the vanilla, orange zest and juice, and egg yolks and continue to beat on medium speed until fully incorporated.

With the mixer set on low speed, beat in the flour, one-third at a time, beating well after each addition. Stir in the pecans. The dough should be soft and light. Cover the bowl and refrigerate the dough until it is slightly chilled, about 30 minutes.

Preheat an oven to 350°F (180°C). Line a baking sheet with parchment paper. Using a teaspoon, scoop up the dough and roll it between the palms of your hands into 1-inch (2.5-cm) balls. Arrange them on the prepared baking sheet, leaving space between each ball.

Bake until golden, about 10 minutes. Remove from the oven and transfer to wire racks to let cool for a few minutes. Roll as many warm cookies as you think will be eaten in confectioners' sugar to coat evenly. Let coated and uncoated cookies cool completely on wire racks before storing.

Mexican Coffee

SERVES 6

Called café de olla *and traditionally served in pottery mugs, this spice-infused coffee complements the wedding cookies. Select a full-bodied, dark-roast coffee for the best results.*

8 cups (64 fl oz/2 l) water
2 cinnamon sticks, each about 2 inches
    (5 cm) long
1 cup (7 oz/220 g) firmly packed
    brown sugar
1 strip orange peel studded with 2
    whole cloves
2 cups (16 fl oz/500 ml) dark-roast
    ground coffee

In a saucepan over high heat, combine the water, cinnamon sticks, brown sugar and clove-studded orange peel. Bring to a boil, stirring to dissolve the sugar. Once the sugar is dissolved, add the coffee and turn off the heat. Cover and let stand for 5 minutes. Strain liquid through a fine-mesh sieve into 6 cups and serve at once.

Mexican Hot Chocolate

SERVES 6

Round tablets of Mexican chocolate are commonly packed into lightweight cardboard packaging and sold in Mexican specialty-food stores and well-stocked markets. Each round is divided into 8 wedges. The chocolate is flavored with sugar and other seasonings, such as vanilla and cinnamon, and has a slightly gritty texture. In Mexico the chocolate, once it has melted in the hot milk or water, is beaten with a carved wooden molinillo *until very frothy. An electric mixer or whisk can be used in its place.*

3 cups (24 fl oz/750 ml) milk or water
3 wedges (3 oz/90 g each) Mexican
    chocolate, crumbled

In a saucepan over medium heat, warm the milk or water until small bubbles form along the edge of the pan. Add the chocolate and stir until it melts, then simmer gently for a few minutes to blend the flavors. Now beat with a *molinillo,* an electric mixer set on low speed or a whisk until very frothy and the chocolate melts.

Pour into small cups and serve immediately.

Mexican Wedding Cookies;
Mexican Coffee; Mexican Hot Chocolate

ENGAGEMENT PARTY

IFE SENDS OUR way many happy moments. Today these milestones can be observed with special recognition without the fuss of a more traditional, formal party. Here we celebrate a young couple's engagement by throwing open the doors and serving a filling but easy meal suitable for a small gathering or a large crowd.

We felt buffet-style service starting in mid to late afternoon would suit the leisurely tone of the party and would encourage guests to mingle on into the evening. You could arrange the food on a sideboard in the dining room, or on any table that is large enough to hold oversized platters and serving dishes. Small containers of flowers and clusters of cathedral candles lend a relaxed air. The open-hearted, Spanish feel of this menu makes it adaptable for other occasions, too, such as a house-warming or *bon voyage* party.

WHEN GUESTS ARRIVE for the celebration, they are welcomed with pitchers of ice-cold sangría. Although you can serve it in any glasses that hold a generous amount, we used oversized glass goblets to show off the Spanish wine punch to its most striking effect.

Most of the preparation for the meal is easily done in advance. The recipes can be doubled or tripled for a larger group, but plan on the additional time and expense a bigger affair will demand. We chose to present the paella in a wide rustic earthenware dish, but you can use any serving dish large enough to show off the assortment of seafood and chicken or serve already-plated portions.

Menu

Simple gifts for the engaged couple could range from a set of thick kitchen towels for their new home to fabric-wrapped bottles of wine to help start their bar or wine cellar.

Beverage Ideas

Although sangría (recipe on page 155) can be sipped throughout the meal with satisfaction, a selection of red and white wines is welcome. For the whites, choose more rustic types such as Pouilly Fumé, Sancerre or a simple French Chablis, Italian Vernaccia or American Sauvignon Blanc or Chardonnay. For the reds, select from Spanish Riojas, American Pinot Noirs, Merlots or Syrahs from the Rhône or elsewhere. Chilled kirschwasser would make a fine climax to the meal.

Roasted Eggplant & Peppers

*Asparagus & Beets with
Romesco Mayonnaise*

Simple Country Paella

Sangría

Bing Cherry Cheese Tart

Mussels, clams, shrimp, chicken and saffron-tinted rice transform the surface of a paella into an edible landscape.

Preparation List

❧ The day before, make and freeze the tart shell, cook the beets and make the mayonnaise; roast the eggplants, peppers and the onion(s), if using, and assemble. Marinate the chicken, pit the cherries and prepare the sangría base.

❧ That morning, brown the chicken, assemble the paella base and cook the asparagus. Combine the cherries and the liqueur, make the cheese filling for the tart and prebake the tart shell.

❧ An hour before, assemble and bake the tart and debeard the mussels.

EACH RECIPE YIELDS 6 SERVINGS.

Citrus fruits form a backdrop for goblets of thirst-quenching sangría.

Roasted Eggplant & Peppers

SERVES 6

On another occasion, offer this versatile dish as part of an antipasto spread or an assortment of tapas. It also doubles as a robust topping for bread, in which case you should coarsely chop the eggplants, peppers and onions for easier spreading. Put all of the vegetables into the oven at the same time and then remove them as they are ready. This dish can be assembled the day before, but the salt and vinegar will need to be adjusted to taste just before serving.

2 small eggplants (aubergines)
1 large or 2 small red (Spanish) onions, unpeeled (optional)
3 red bell peppers (capsicums)
olive oil for rubbing on onion(s), plus ½ cup (4 fl oz/125 ml) olive oil
2 teaspoons ground cumin
2 tablespoons sherry vinegar
salt and freshly ground pepper
4 tablespoons chopped fresh flat-leaf (Italian) parsley
handful of sharply flavored black or green olives

*P*reheat an oven to 400°F (200°C).
🌳 Prick the eggplant in a few places with a fork and place in a baking pan. If using the onion(s), rub them with olive oil and add them to the pan. Roast the eggplants, turning occasionally to ensure even cooking, until tender, 35–45 minutes. Set aside until cool enough to handle. Continue to roast the onion(s), until tender when pierced with a knife, about 50 minutes, then set aside to cool.
🌳 To roast the peppers, preheat a broiler (griller). Place the peppers on a baking sheet and slip under the broiler.

Broil (grill), turning occasionally, until the skins are evenly blackened and blistered. Transfer to a closed paper bag or plastic container and let stand until cool enough to handle, about 10 minutes.
🌳 Using your fingers, peel off the charred skin from the peppers. Cut the peppers in half and pull out and discard the stems, seeds and ribs. Cut the peppers into long, thin strips. Peel the eggplants and cut the flesh into 1½–2-inch (4–5-cm) cubes. Place in a colander to drain. Then peel the onion(s) and cut into long, thin strips. Set aside.
🌳 Combine the drained eggplant, the bell peppers and onion(s) in a large bowl. In a small bowl, whisk together the ½ cup (4 fl oz/125 ml) olive oil, cumin and sherry vinegar and toss the vegetables with the mixture. Season to taste with salt and pepper.
🌳 At serving time, garnish with the parsley and olives.

*M*arketed in a range of shapes and in hues from white to purple-black, an assortment of eggplants is available in today's produce markets.

Asparagus & Beets with Romesco Mayonnaise

SERVES 6

Beets and asparagus with a spicy tomato-almond mayonnaise are a wonderful beginning to a meal. If asparagus are out of season, use green beans in their place. To transform this dish into a main course, add cooked potatoes to the assortment. The beets can be either baked or boiled. They can be cooked and the Romesco mayonnaise made 1 day in advance. The asparagus can be cooked 4 hours ahead of serving.

FOR THE ROMESCO MAYONNAISE:

1 tablespoon minced garlic
coarse salt
1½ cups (12 fl oz/375 ml) mayonnaise
1 cup (4 oz/125 g) sliced almonds, toasted and chopped (see page 185)
½ cup (3 oz/90 g) seeded and finely chopped, drained canned plum (Roma) tomatoes
½ teaspoon cayenne pepper
¼ cup (2 fl oz/60 ml) tomato purée
¼ cup (2 fl oz/60 ml) red wine vinegar
salt and freshly ground pepper to taste

1½ lb (750 g) asparagus
12 small beets (beetroots)

*T*o make the Romesco mayonnaise, in a mortar, combine the garlic with a little coarse salt and, using a pestle, grind them together to form a paste. Alternatively, in a bowl and using a fork or the back of a spoon, mash together the garlic and salt to form a paste. Place the mayonnaise in a bowl and stir in the garlic paste. Fold in the almonds, tomatoes, cayenne pepper, tomato purée, vinegar and salt and pepper to taste until well mixed. Cover and refrigerate.

Roasted Eggplant & Peppers; Asparagus & Beets with Romesco Mayonnaise

🌳 Break off the tough ends of the asparagus where they snap easily and trim the spears to a uniform length. If the stalks are thick, peel them with a paring knife or vegetable peeler.

🌳 Half fill a large, wide frying pan with salted water and bring to a boil. Add the asparagus and boil until tender-crisp, 4–6 minutes; the timing will depend upon the thickness of the stalks. Drain well and immerse immediately in ice water to stop the cooking and set the color. Drain well again and pat dry.

🌳 To bake the beets, preheat an oven to 375°F (190°C). Trim the greens off the beets but leave about ½ inch (12 mm) of the stems intact. Scrub the beets and wrap them together in aluminum foil, sealing tightly. Place in a baking dish and add water to a depth of 1–2 inches (2.5–5 cm). Bake until tender when pierced with a knife, about 1 hour, adding additional water to the pan as needed to make steam. Remove from the oven, let cool and then remove and discard the foil. Peel the beets and cut into wedges.

🌳 Alternatively, to boil the beets, trim as directed. Bring a saucepan three-fourths full of water to a boil. Add the beets and boil until tender, 30–40 minutes. Drain well and immerse in warm water. When cool enough to handle, peel the beets and cut into wedges.

🌳 To serve, place the beets and asparagus on a platter. Pass the mayonnaise in a bowl. Or arrange the vegetables on individual plates and garnish each plate with a dollop of the mayonnaise.

Simple Country Paella; Sangria

Simple Country Paella

SERVES 6

Paella need not be an elaborate and expensive dish. Some of the very best versions are the simplest. Of course you can add chunks of diced ham or chorizo, or shrimp, but the dish will be satisfying even without these embellishments. Begin marinating the chicken the day before. Four hours before, brown the chicken and cook the onion, garlic and tomato base in the same pan. The rest of the dish must be done at the last minute, but why not sip sangría and talk with your guests while you cook and stir?

FOR THE MARINADE:

2 tablespoons minced garlic
2 tablespoons dried oregano, crumbled
2 teaspoons salt
1 tablespoon coarsely ground pepper
3–4 tablespoons red wine vinegar
5–6 tablespoons (2½–3 fl oz/75–90 ml) olive oil

12 small half chicken breasts, or 6 small chicken thighs and 6 small half chicken breasts
¼ cup (2 fl oz/60 ml) dry white wine or water, plus dry white wine or water for cooking clams or mussels
½ teaspoon saffron threads
6 tablespoons (3 fl oz/90 ml) olive oil
2 large yellow onions, chopped
1 tablespoon minced garlic
3–4 cups (18–24 oz/560–750 g) seeded and diced canned plum (Roma) tomatoes
2 cups (14 oz/440 g) short-grain white rice
4–5 cups (32–40 fl oz/1–1.25 l) chicken stock
24 shrimp (prawns), peeled and deveined (optional)
1 cup (5 oz/155 g) shelled peas or tender, young lima beans

36 clams and/or mussels in the shell, scrubbed and debearded if using mussels

To make the marinade, in a small bowl, combine the garlic, oregano, salt and pepper. Add the vinegar and stir to form a paste. Stir in the olive oil.

❧ Place the chicken pieces in a glass or plastic container. Rub the marinade on the chicken pieces, coating evenly. Cover and refrigerate overnight.

❧ In a small saucepan over low heat, warm the ¼ cup (2 fl oz/60 ml) wine or water; remove from the heat. Crush the saffron threads gently and add to the warm liquid. Let stand for 10 minutes.

❧ In a large, deep frying pan over medium-high heat, warm the olive oil. Add the chicken in batches and brown quickly on all sides. Remove from the pan and set aside. To the oil remaining in the pan, add the onions and sauté over medium heat, stirring often, until tender and translucent, about 10 minutes. Add the garlic and tomatoes and sauté, stirring, for 5 minutes.

❧ Add the rice, reduce the heat to low and stir for 3 minutes. Add the chicken stock (the amount you add will depend on the absorbency of the rice) and the saffron and its soaking liquid and bring to a boil. Reduce the heat and simmer, uncovered and without stirring, for 10 minutes. Add the browned chicken and continue to cook, uncovered, until the liquids are absorbed and the rice is tender, about 10 minutes longer, adding the shrimp, if using, and the peas or lima beans during the last 5 minutes. Alternatively, once the chicken is added, place the pan in an oven preheated to 325°F (165°C) and bake until the liquids are absorbed and the rice is tender, about 15 minutes, adding the

shrimp and peas or lima beans during the last 5 minutes.

❧ Meanwhile, in a saucepan, place the clams and/or mussels, discarding any that do not close to the touch. Add wine or water to a depth of 1 inch (2.5 cm). Cover, place over medium-high heat and cook until the shellfish open, about 5 minutes. Add them to the paella 1–2 minutes before it is ready, discarding any that did not open.

❧ Remove the paella from the stove top or oven and let rest for 10 minutes before serving.

Sangría

SERVES 6

A wine punch popular in Spain as well as Portugal, especially during the hot summer months. Combining the wine, sugar, lemons and oranges the night before serving intensifies the flavors.

1 bottle (3 cups/24 fl oz/750 ml) dry red wine such as Rioja
3 tablespoons sugar
2–3 tablespoons fresh lemon juice
½ cup (4 fl oz/125 ml) fresh orange juice
2 lemons, thinly sliced
2 oranges, thinly sliced
3–4 cups (24–32 fl oz/750 ml–1 l) club soda
ice cubes

In a glass bowl or other nonreactive container, stir togther the wine, sugar, and lemon and orange juices and slices. Cover and refrigerate overnight to blend the flavors.

❧ At serving time, transfer the wine mixture to 1 or 2 pitchers. Add the club soda and plenty of ice cubes.

Bing Cherry Cheese Tart

SERVES 6, WITH LEFTOVERS

The tart shell can be made 1 or 2 days ahead and frozen. The cherries can be pitted the night before and refrigerated; combine them with the liqueur 4 hours before assembling the tart. The cheese mixture can be assembled at the same time. Serve the tart slightly warm or at room temperature.

2 cups (8 oz/250 g) stemmed Bing cherries, pitted, or raspberries or blueberries

2 tablespoons Tuaca, amaretto or Frangelico

FOR THE TART SHELL:

1¼ cups (6½ oz/200 g) all-purpose (plain) flour

¼ cup (2 oz/60 g) sugar

½ cup (4 oz/125 g) unsalted butter, chilled, cut into slivers

1 egg yolk

2 tablespoons heavy (double) cream

1 tablespoon Tuaca, amaretto or Frangelico

1 teaspoon finely grated lemon zest (see page 185)

FOR THE CHEESE TOPPING:

1 cup (8 oz/250 g) cream cheese at room temperature

⅓ cup (3 oz/90 g) sugar

2 whole eggs or 1 whole egg and 2 egg yolks

2 tablespoons Tuaca, amaretto or Frangelico

½ teaspoon almond extract (essence)

In a bowl, toss together the cherries and liqueur. Cover and let stand for 4 hours to blend the flavors.

To make the tart shell pastry by hand, in a bowl, stir together the flour and sugar. Drop the butter into the bowl and, using two knives or a pastry blender, cut in the butter until the mixture resembles cornmeal. In a small bowl, whisk together the egg yolk, cream, liqueur and lemon zest. Add to the flour mixture and, using a fork, stir together until the dough forms a rough mass. Gather the dough into a ball, flatten it, and wrap in plastic wrap. Chill for 1 hour or for up to 1 day. (If the dough has been chilling for a day, allow it to soften a bit before rolling it out.)

To make the tart shell pastry in a food processor, place the flour and sugar in a processor fitted with the metal blade. Add the butter pieces and, using rapid on-off pulses, process until the mixture resembles cornmeal. In a small bowl, whisk together the egg yolk, cream, liqueur and lemon zest. Add to the flour and process briefly just until the dough forms a rough mass, then gather, shape, wrap and chill as for hand method.

Preheat an oven to 400°F (200°C). On a well-floured surface, roll out the dough into a round about 11 inches (28 cm) in diameter. Carefully transfer the round to a 9-inch (23-cm) tart pan with a removable bottom. Alternatively, if the dough is difficult to roll out, press by hand into the tart tin. In either case, do not fit the dough too snugly to the pan, as the crust will shrink as it bakes. Make the sides slightly higher than the tart rim, so that there will be enough of an edge to hold the filling. Trim off any excess overhang.

Using a fork, prick a few holes in the bottom of the crust. Line the tart shell with aluminum foil and fill with pie weights or beans. Bake for 15 minutes, then remove the foil and weights. Lower the oven temperature to 350°F (180°C) and bake for about 15 minutes longer. Transfer to a wire rack to cool for about 15 minutes. Leave the oven set at 350°F (180°C).

Meanwhile, to make the cheese filling, in a bowl combine the cream cheese, sugar, whole eggs or whole egg and egg yolks, liqueur and almond extract. Using an electric mixer set on medium, beat until well combined. Alternatively, place the ingredients in a food processor fitted with the metal blade and process until well combined.

Distribute the cherries evenly on the bottom of the tart shell. Pour the cheese mixture over the cherries. Bake until the custard is set, about 25 minutes. Cool on a wire rack.

To pit summertime's fresh cherries easily, use a cherry pitter, which holds the fruit and pushes out the pit when pressure is applied.

Bing Cherry Cheese Tart

WEEKEND CARD PARTY

A WEEKEND CARD PARTY is the ideal opportunity for old friends or new acquaintances to come together. This gathering has been designed with a great deal of latitude, however, making it easily transformable into a baby shower, an informal committee meeting or a casual reunion. Indeed, the menu will suit any occasion that calls for spending an afternoon in leisurely but stylish fashion with food suited to a late brunch, lunch or early dinner.

We opted for an airy pink-and-green color scheme. Using pinking shears, we quickly gave decorative edges to lengths of patterned fabric for the tablecloth and napkins and placed them on top of a white tablecloth. You could use any colorful tablecoth. We set the table in a bright, sunny alcove and used imaginative floral touches around the room to achieve the feeling of an indoor garden party.

Gentle pastels and garden motifs repeated in Italian pottery place settings, tablecloth, napkin rings and napkins contribute to the atmosphere of an indoor garden party.

Menu

OUR CARD PARTY for four was planned to keep the host or hostess out of the kitchen as much as possible. Reheating the soup, broiling the cheese-and-tapenade sandwiches and quickly pan-frying the crab cakes are the only tasks that need to be done while the party is in progress. The soup can be presented in a tureen and the sandwiches can be piled on platters for buffet-style service. Quantities can be doubled or tripled for a larger group.

Both desserts can be made up to a day ahead of time. Festive yet simple, they may be savored as the afternoon activities unwind.

Let guests help themselves from a side table set with goblets, wine and sparkling and still mineral waters. Provide a small dish of lemon slices and a bowl or bucket of ice for guests who wish to mix spritzers, using equal amounts of white wine and sparkling water.

Red Pepper & Tomato Soup

Waldorf Chicken Salad Sandwiches

Grilled Cheese & Tapenade Sandwiches

Crab Cake & Red Rémoulade Rolls

Old-Fashioned Brownies

Cold Lemon Soufflé

Preparation List

❧ Make the tapenade one week or up to two weeks before the party.

❧ A couple of days before, make the soup.

❧ Cook the chicken, make the rémoulade and bake the brownies the day before. Prepare the crab cake mixture and form into cakes.

❧ Make and chill the soufflé the night before the party so that it will be well chilled.

❧ In the morning, make the chicken salad.

❧ An hour before, assemble the sandwiches.

EACH RECIPE YIELDS 4 SERVINGS.

Beverage Ideas

Offer assorted beers, classic cocktails, such as martinis and old-fashioneds, and, for those who worry about their skill and bets, citrus-flavored mineral waters and ginger ale. For wines, pour Sauvignon Blanc, French Mâcon-Villages or Italian Pinot Grigio for the white. A zesty rosé would be nice, too.

Regardless of who holds the winning hand, you could reward your guests with a few inexpensive party favors. Here, a picture frame, pencil holder and notebook all sport a playing-card motif.

Red Pepper & Tomato Soup

SERVES 4, WITH LEFTOVERS

Chili powder and a cilantro garnish give this brightly colored soup a subtle south-of-the-border character. You could also garnish the soup with sour cream or crème fraîche and a little minced jalapeño, if the added heat appeals.

For a smooth soup, pass the tomato mixture through a food mill or coarse-mesh sieve twice; for a chunkier texture, pass it though just once. The soup can be prepared up to 2 days ahead and then reheated over medium heat just before serving. If vine-ripened tomatoes are unavailable, canned plum (Roma) tomatoes can be used, but the soup will take on a different personality.

2 tablespoons olive oil
1 yellow onion, chopped
2 teaspoons chili powder
pinch of cayenne pepper, optional
1 lb (500 g) red bell peppers (capsi-
    cums), seeded, deribbed and diced
1 lb (500 g) tomatoes, diced
2–3 cups (16–24 fl oz/500–750 ml)
    water or chicken stock
salt and freshly ground pepper
chopped fresh cilantro (fresh coriander)
sour cream or crème fraîche, optional
minced fresh jalapeño (hot green) chili
    peppers, optional

*I*n a large saucepan over medium heat, warm the olive oil. Add the onion and sauté until tender and translucent, about 8 minutes. Add the chili powder and the cayenne, if using, and sauté 1–2 minutes longer. Add the bell peppers, tomatoes and 2 cups (16 fl oz/500 ml) water or stock. Bring to a boil over high heat and simmer, uncovered, until the peppers are soft and the tomatoes have given off their liquids, about 15–20 minutes. Add the remaining 1 cup (8 fl oz/250 ml) water or stock if the mixture is very thick.

Working in batches, pass the mixture through a food mill or coarse-mesh sieve placed over a clean saucepan to remove the seeds and skins. You will have a somewhat coarse purée. For a smoother texture, pass the mixture though the food mill or sieve again.

Bring to a simmer over medium heat, then taste and adjust the seasoning with salt and pepper. Serve garnished with cilantro and with sour cream or crème fraîche and jalapeños, if you like.

Red Pepper & Tomato Soup

Waldorf Chicken Salad Sandwiches

Waldorf Chicken Salad Sandwiches

SERVES 4

Nearly everyone loves a Waldorf salad, with its crunch of walnuts and celery and sweet-tart apples. Why not add chicken and bread and serve a great chicken salad sandwich? The chicken can be cooked up to 1 day in advance. The recipe includes directions for poaching the breasts but you can sauté them in olive oil or broil (grill) them if you prefer. The salad can be assembled up to 8 hours before the party begins. The sandwiches can be made, wrapped in plastic wrap and refrigerated 2 hours before the party; bring to room temperature before serving.

4 half chicken breasts, boned
   (5–6 oz/155–185 g each)
chicken stock, to cover
¾ cup (6 fl oz/180 ml) mayonnaise
2 teaspoons finely grated orange zest
   (see page 185)
3 tablespoons fresh orange juice
1 large Granny Smith or other tart
   green apple, peeled, cored and cut
   into ¼-inch (6-mm) dice
3 celery stalks, cut into ¼-inch
   (6-mm) dice
⅓ cup (1½ oz/45 g) walnuts, toasted
   and chopped (see page 185)
8 standard slices fine-textured bread or
   4 large pita bread rounds
watercress sprigs

*P*lace the chicken breast halves side by side in a sauté pan and add chicken stock to cover. Bring to a simmer over medium heat and simmer until cooked through, 8–10 minutes. Using a slotted spoon, transfer the breasts to a work surface. Let cool, then cut into ½-inch (12-mm) or smaller dice.

🌳 In a small bowl, stir together the mayonnaise and orange zest and juice.

🌳 In another, larger bowl, combine the diced chicken, apple, celery and walnuts. Add the mayonnaise and toss to coat all the ingredients evenly.

🌳 Spread the chicken salad on half of the bread slices. Lay 2 or 3 watercress sprigs on the salad and then top each with a second slice. Cut in half. Alternatively, cut the pita rounds in half and open each half carefully. Gently tuck 2 or 3 watercress sprigs and then some of the chicken salad into each half.

Your best local bakery will yield a wide variety of loaves and rolls suitable for the menu's assorted sandwiches.

Grilled Cheese & Tapenade Sandwiches

SERVES 4

If you want to serve this open-faced, grilled cheese sandwich closed, use softer bread and sauté in unsalted butter on a griddle or in a large sauté pan (see below). The tapenade can be prepared up to 2 weeks before the party. The sandwiches can be assembled 2 hours before serving and then slipped under the broiler at the last moment. Add tomato slices to the sandwiches only if full-flavored tomatoes are in the market. The number of slices you need will depend upon the sandwich size. The cheese slices should be cut the same dimensions as the bread slices.

¾ cup (6 fl oz/180 ml) tapenade (recipe on page 182)
8 slices French or Italian bread
4 large or 8 small tomato slices, optional
8 thin slices Fontina cheese

𝒫reheat a broiler (griller). Spread the tapenade on the bread slices. Top each slice with 1 or 2 tomato slices, if using, and then with a slice of Fontina. Gently place the sandwiches on a baking sheet or broiler pan.

🌳 Slip under the broiler and broil (grill) until the cheese melts, 1–2 minutes. If the slices are large, cut in half. Serve warm.

Closed Sandwiches

To make closed sandwiches, spread the tapenade on the bread slices. On 4 of the slices, layer a piece of cheese, the tomato slices, if using, and another piece of cheese.

🌳 Top with the remaining bread slices. On a griddle or in a large sauté pan over medium heat, melt unsalted butter. Add the sandwiches and weight them down with a pot lid. When they are golden on the first side, turn them and cook until golden brown on the second side, about 4–5 minutes total cooking time.

Crab Cake & Red Rémoulade Rolls

SERVES 4

A warm crab cake (see recipe on page 16) tucked into a soft roll or bun and slathered with rémoulade sauce is a great sandwich for an informal party. You can make the rémoulade and form the crab cakes 1 day in advance of the party and then fry them just before serving. This rémoulade departs from the traditional recipe in its lack of anchovy and its addition of tomato paste, which imparts a lovely rose hue.

4 crab cakes (recipe on page 16)

FOR THE RED RÉMOULADE:

1 cup (8 fl oz/250 ml) mayonnaise
1 tablespoon Dijon mustard
1½ tablespoons tomato paste
3 tablespoons minced white onion
3 tablespoons chopped cornichons
1 tablespoon chopped well-drained capers
2 tablespoons chopped fresh flat-leaf (Italian) parsley
½ teaspoon freshly ground pepper
brine from the cornichons
salt

4 buns or soft rolls, split and warmed
3 cups (6 oz/185 g) torn romaine (cos) lettuce or watercress sprigs

𝒫repare the crab cake mixture and form into 4 cakes, each about ½ inch (12 mm) thick.

🌳 To make the red rémoulade, in a bowl stir together the mayonnaise, mustard, tomato paste, onion, cornichons, capers, parsley, pepper and the cornichon brine and salt to taste.

🌳 Spread the cut side of each bun or roll with rémoulade. Fry the crab cakes as directed. Add the romaine lettuce or watercress to one side of each bun or roll and top with a hot crab cake. Top with the remaining bun or roll halves and serve immediately.

Old-Fashioned Brownies

MAKES 12

These brownies can be baked 1 day in advance of serving and stored in a covered container at room temperature.

3 oz (90 g) unsweetened chocolate

6 tablespoons (3 oz/90 g) unsalted butter

1 teaspoon vanilla extract (essence)

3 eggs

¼ teaspoon salt

1 cup (8 oz/250 g) sugar

¾ cup (4 oz/125 g) all-purpose (plain) flour

¾ cup (3 oz/90 g) walnuts, toasted and chopped (see page 185)

Preheat an oven to 350°F (180°C). Butter and flour an 8- or 9-inch (20- or 23-cm) square baking pan.

🌳 Place the chocolate and butter in the top pan of a double boiler or in a heat-proof bowl. Set over (but not touching) hot water and stir until melted. Stir in the vanilla and remove from the hot water. Set aside.

🌳 In a bowl, using an electric mixer set on medium speed, beat the eggs and salt until the eggs are fully blended. Add the sugar, beating constantly, until the mixture is light and fluffy. Fold in the melted chocolate and then the flour and nuts. Pour into the prepared pan.

🌳 Bake until the brownies are shiny on top, shrink away from the sides of the pan, and a wooden skewer inserted in the center comes out covered with moist crumbs, about 25 minutes. Transfer to a wire rack and let cool completely in the pan. Cut into squares to serve.

Old-Fashioned Brownies; Cold Lemon Soufflé

Cold Lemon Soufflé

SERVES 4

Because this light dessert looks more difficult to prepare than it actually is, it makes a great impression. An easy and delicious version of the traditional airy dessert, you can still create the illusion of a risen soufflé by wrapping and tying a buttered aluminum foil collar on a 3-cup (24 fl oz / 750 ml) soufflé dish or onto small individual soufflé dishes. If the illusion is not important to you, simply pour the lemon soufflé mixture into dessert ramekins or an attractive 1-quart (1-l) bowl. This dessert can be made the night before, covered and then refrigerated. It can also be frozen for up to 2 weeks and thawed in the refrigerator when needed, making it an ideal dessert for drop-in guests or a tasty midnight snack.

1 tablespoon plain gelatin
¼ cup (2 fl oz / 60 ml) water
4 eggs, separated, at room temperature
½ cup (4 fl oz / 125 ml) fresh lemon juice
1 cup (8 oz / 250 g) sugar
pinch of salt
finely grated zest of 1 lemon (see page 185)
1 cup (8 fl oz / 250 ml) heavy (double) cream
raspberries, strawberries or strips of lemon peel, optional

*I*n a small bowl, sprinkle the gelatin over the water and let stand to soften without stirring, about 3 minutes.

🌳 In a small enameled or stainless steel saucepan, whisk together the egg yolks, lemon juice, ½ cup (4 oz / 125 g) of the sugar and the salt. Cook over very low heat, whisking constantly, until thickened, about 5 minutes. Remove from the heat.

🌳 Add the gelatin mixture and whisk until dissolved and well blended. Stir in the lemon zest. Pour into a large bowl, cover and refrigerate while you beat the egg whites and cream.

🌳 In a bowl, beat the egg whites until soft peaks form. Gradually beat in the remaining ½ cup (4 oz / 125 g) sugar and beat until stiff peaks form.

🌳 In a large chilled bowl with chilled beaters, beat the cream until stiff peaks form. Using a rubber spatula, fold the egg whites into the whipped cream just until combined. Stir one-third of the cream mixture into the lemon custard base to lighten it. Gently fold in the remaining cream–egg whites mixture just until no streaks of white remain.

🌳 Pour the soufflé mixture into a collared soufflé dish or dishes or into a bowl or individual ramekins (see note). Cover and chill for at least 4–6 hours or for up to 1 day. Garnish with berries or strips of lemon peel, if desired.

Decks of cards, score pads and pencils stand ready for an afternoon's entertainment once dessert and coffee have been served.

CASUAL PIZZA PARTY

$\mathcal{W}$HAT COULD BE more casual than letting your guests assemble and cook their own food? Many people love to participate in making a pizza, and the method we chose for this menu is well within anyone's culinary abilities.

Such an occasion is best suited to a weekend afternoon or early evening, when guests have more time to join in. With so many people preparing their pizzas, it makes good sense to set the event in the kitchen or as close to the kitchen as possible. If you have a large enough kitchen, make the pizzas in there and then serve them with the rest of the meal in an informal dining room; but, if the kitchen has a dining area, you could have seating there. After preparing the pizzas everyone could gather in the family room to watch a movie or sporting event on television, in which case, you might arrange chairs, tables and trays around the set.

A LTHOUGH YOUR GUESTS will do much of the final food compilation, you still have to make the pizza dough, sauces and toppings. The work is time-consuming, but it can be spread out over a couple of weeks. If you're pressed for time, you can prepare only as many of the toppings suggested on page 174 as seem manageable. A whimsical salad accompanies the pizzas, and *biscotti* and fruit end the meal in similarly relaxed style.

Provide a wide variety of beers and soft drinks on ice for guests to choose from. Use your imagination to create an ice chest from whatever container you have on hand, just be sure to line it with plastic first. We placed some large goblets nearby, but any tall glass will do.

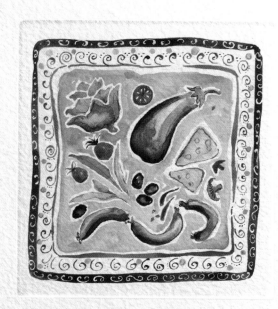

Menu

Cluster extra aprons and cooking utensils within easy reach for guests who wish to participate in the cooking.

Beverage Ideas

Offer a wide array of beers, assembling an assortment of styles (pilsners, lagers, ales and stouts) and countries. Pour medium-bodied Italian reds, such as Chianti, Rosso di Montalcino and Nebbiolo, for the wine drinkers and nonalcoholic beers and a selection of soft drinks and mineral waters for the nondrinkers.

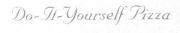

Do-It-Yourself Pizza

Insalata Capricciosa

Macedonia di Frutta

Hazelnut Biscotti

Terra-cotta plates, sturdy tumblers and colorful table linens complement the bright palette of pizza ingredients.

Preparation List

❧ Make the tapenade up to two weeks before and the pesto and the sun-dried tomato spread up to one week before.

❧ During the week, make the *biscotti*.

❧ The day before, make the tomato purée and the cooked pizza toppings.

❧ In the morning, make the pizza dough and vinaigrette. Wash and crisp the lettuce and ready the vegetables for the salad.

❧ Prepare the uncooked pizza toppings and make the *macedonia* a few hours before.

❧ One and one-half hours before, marinate the chick-peas for the salad.

EACH RECIPE YIELDS 6 SERVINGS.

Instead of a standard cooler, we used a large terra-cotta pot for icing beers and soft drinks, but any large container lined with plastic and filled with ice may be substituted.

Do-It-Yourself Pizza

This is a versatile recipe. Prepare as many of the suggested spreads and toppings as you like. The topping amounts given are conservative suggestions and should be enough to top 12 small pizzas with an assortment of ingredients. If your guests favor certain ingredients, have plenty of those on hand. Judge and adjust according to your own personal tastes and those of the party goers—if you know them.

The tapenade can be made up to 2 weeks in advance. The pesto and sun-dried tomato spread can be made up to 1 week in advance and the tomato purée can be made up to 2 days in advance. Prepare the cooked toppings 1 day in advance and cut the uncooked ones 4 hours before the party.

A sponge is a type of starter that gives a particularly resilient texture to the crust. The addition of rye or buckwheat flour to the dough deepens the flavor of the crust. The dough can be made 8 hours before the party, left to rise at room temperature, and then divided into 12 equal portions, covered with plastic wrap and refrigerated. Remove the dough balls from the refrigerator about 30 minutes before forming them into crusts.

If you have one or two baking stones, place them in the oven when you turn it on; the stones will ensure a crisp crust. You will need a baker's peel or a rimless baking sheet to slide the pizzas onto the stone.

When it is time for the guests to top their pizzas, set out all the spreads and toppings in bowls or on platters and let the guests choose from among them.

This recipe yields 12 small pizzas; bake 6 pizzas at a time so everyone eats together.

SUGGESTED SPREADS FOR THE CRUST:

tapenade (recipe on page 182)

pesto (recipe on page 183)

sun-dried tomato spread (recipe on page 182)

tomato purée (recipe on page 183)

SUGGESTED TOPPINGS:

4 medium-sized red (Spanish) onions, sliced and lightly sautéed

4 large red or green bell peppers (capsicums), seeded, deribbed, sliced and lightly sautéed

1 lb (500 g) fresh mushrooms, sliced and lightly sautéed

1 lb (500 g) small new potatoes, roasted and sliced ¼ inch (6 mm) thick

2 eggplants (aubergines), sliced ¼ inch (6 mm) thick and baked or grilled

2 lb (1 kg) escarole or Swiss chard, chopped, lightly sautéed and well drained

1 lb (500 g) Italian sausages, cooked and then sliced

½ lb (250 g) sliced *pancetta*, cut into strips and sautéed

1½ lbs (750 g) tomatoes, diced and drained

2 cups (8 oz/250 g) freshly grated Parmesan cheese

1 lb (500 g) fresh mozzarella cheese, sliced

¾ lb (375 g) Fontina cheese, shredded or sliced

FOR THE SPONGE:

3 tablespoons active dry yeast

1½ cups (12 fl oz/375 ml) warm (110°F/43°C) water

1½ cups (7½ oz/235 g) unbleached all-purpose (plain) flour

FOR THE DOUGH:

2¼ cups (18 fl oz/560 ml) warm (110°F/43°C) water

½ cup (4 fl oz/125 ml) plus 1 tablespoon olive oil

1 tablespoon salt

9 cups (2¾ lb/1.4 kg) unbleached all-purpose (plain) flour, plus additional flour as needed

1 cup (3 oz/90 g) rye or buckwheat flour or 1 additional cup (5 oz/155 g) all-purpose (plain) flour

½ cup (¾ oz/20 g) finely chopped rosemary or sage

cornmeal for baking sheets

olive oil for brushing on crust, optional

*S*elect and prepare the spreads and the toppings for the pizzas.

🌳 To make the sponge, in a heavy-duty electric mixer fitted with a paddle attachment, dissolve the yeast in the warm water. Add the flour and beat at medium speed until all the ingredients are fully combined. (Or combine the ingredients in a large bowl and mix with a wooden spoon.) Cover the bowl with a dampened kitchen towel or plastic wrap and let rest in a warm, draft-free place for 30 minutes.

🌳 To make the dough, add the warm water, olive oil, salt, flour(s) and rosemary or sage to the sponge. Beat with the paddle attachment until all the ingredients come together and are well mixed. Then attach the dough hook and beat until the dough pulls away from the sides of the bowl and is smooth and elastic, 5–10 minutes, adding more flour as necessary to reduce stickiness.

🌳 Turn out the dough onto a lightly floured work surface and knead for 1–2 minutes to be sure it has achieved the proper consistency. (Or add the ingredients to the sponge and beat with a wooden spoon until well mixed, then turn out onto a floured surface and knead until smooth and elastic, 15–20 minutes, adding more flour as needed to reduce stickiness.)

🌳 Shape the dough into a ball, place in a lightly oiled bowl, and turn the dough to coat all surfaces with the oil. Cover with a dampened kitchen towel or plastic wrap and let rise in a warm, draft-free place until doubled in size, about 1 hour.

🌳 Turn out the dough onto a lightly floured work surface. Punch down the dough and divide it into 12 equal portions; shape each portion into a ball. Place the balls on a baking sheet, cover with plastic wrap and refrigerate for 30 minutes or for up to 8 hours (see note).

🌳 Preheat an oven to 475°F (245°C).

🌳 To form the crusts, punch down a dough portion one at a time on a lightly floured work surface. Flatten it into a disk about 3 inches (7.5 cm) in diameter. Then, using your fingers and the heels of your hands, gently press and stretch the dough into a 4–5-inch (10–13-cm) round about ¼ inch (6 mm) thick. The edges of the dough round should be a little thicker than the center. Lift the dough round occasionally as you work, to prevent sticking.

🌳 Dust 2 large baking sheets with cornmeal and transfer 6 of the pizza crusts to them. Have the bowls of spreads and toppings ready. Encourage each guest to top his or her own pizza according to their own individual taste.

🌳 Bake the pizzas until the crusts are golden brown, 12–15 minutes. Remove from the oven, brush the edges of the crusts with olive oil, if using, and serve immediately.

Do-It-Yourself Pizza

Insalata Capricciosa

Insalata Capricciosa

SERVES 6

The perfect salad for a do-it-yourself pizza party. Capricciosa more or less means "with whimsy," so use your imagination when putting this salad together. Start with romaine and then add whatever you like, such as diced cucumbers, sliced carrots, cooked chick-peas, a few olives. If you like, cut the carrots into narrow, thin strips rather than slices. If only thick-skinned cucumbers are available, peel them. You can also use canned chick-peas in place of home-cooked ones; rinse and drain them well before adding to the salad. Mix the chick-peas well with a garlicky vinaigrette and add a few croutons (see Green Salad with Gruyère & Croutons, page 66), if desired. You can make the vinaigrette, wash and crisp the lettuce and cut the vegetables 8 hours before serving. Combine the chick-peas and the vinaigrette 1½ hours before serving.

FOR THE GARLIC VINAIGRETTE:

⅔ cup (5 fl oz/160 ml) mild olive oil

⅓ cup (3 fl oz/80 ml) extra-virgin olive oil

¼ cup (2 fl oz/60 ml) red wine vinegar

1 tablespoon balsamic vinegar, optional

2 teaspoons minced garlic

salt and freshly ground pepper

1½–2 cups (9–12 oz/280–375 g) drained, cooked chick-peas (garbanzo beans)

1 small head cauliflower, cut into florets (optional)

12 cups (1½ lb/750 g) torn romaine (cos) lettuce

2 cups (10 oz/315 g) seeded, diced English (hothouse) cucumber

1 cup (4 oz/125 g) thinly sliced carrot

To make the vinaigrette, in a small bowl, whisk together the mild and extra-virgin olive oils, wine vinegar, balsamic vinegar (if using), garlic and salt and pepper to taste. Set aside.

🌳 Place the chick-peas in a bowl and add ½ cup (4 fl oz/125 ml) of the vinaigrette. Stir to coat the chick-peas well and let marinate for 1½ hours. Set the remaining vinaigrette aside.

🌳 If using the cauliflower florets, bring a saucepan three-fourths full of water to a boil. Add the florets and boil until tender-crisp, 3–5 minutes. Drain well and immerse in ice water to cool completely. Drain well again and pat dry with paper towels.

🌳 In a large salad bowl, combine the lettuce, cucumber, carrot, chick-peas and the cauliflower, if using. Drizzle the remaining vinaigrette over the top, toss well and serve.

Flower pots in various shapes and sizes, glued or arranged together on a board (see page 189), form an innovative container for a mostly edible centerpiece of fresh herbs, mushrooms, cherry tomatoes and baby carrots.

Macedonia di Frutta

SERVES 6, WITH LEFTOVERS

After a filling meal of pizza and a hearty salad, a light fruit dessert such as this Italian macedonia is all that is needed. The Italians love to flood this favorite dolce with injudicious amounts of maraschino liqueur, but you may enhance it with the liqueur of your choice; Grand Marnier or kirsch is nice. Or you can omit the alcohol altogether. The macedonia must be prepared 4 hours before serving to allow the flavors to blend. Do not, however, prepare it further than 8 hours ahead, as the fruits will lose their crispness. Any leftovers are great for breakfast.

3 apples, peeled, cored and diced
3 pears, peeled, cored and diced
3 bananas, sliced
2 cups (8 oz/250 g) strawberries, stems
　removed and sliced
2 or 3 oranges, peeled and sectioned
2 cups (16 fl oz/500 ml) fresh orange
　juice
1 cup (8 fl oz/250 ml) fresh lemon juice
¼ cup (2 fl oz/60 ml) orange-flavored
　liqueur, optional
sugar

In a large attractive bowl, combine the fruits, orange and lemon juices, orange liqueur (if using) and sugar to taste. Toss gently to mix well.

🌳 Cover bowl and refrigerate for at least 4 hours or for up to 8 hours, but not longer. Serve chilled.

Hazelnut Biscotti

MAKES 18–20

These cookies can be made 3–5 days before the party and stored in an airtight container. If they soften before serving, recrisp them in a 250°F (120°C) oven. Savor them with espresso, tea or dessert wine.

2½ cups (12½ oz/390 g) all-purpose
　(plain) flour
1½ teaspoons baking powder
½ teaspoon salt
1 teaspoon ground cinnamon
½ cup (4 oz/125 g) unsalted butter at
　room temperature
1 cup (8 oz/250 g) sugar
3 eggs
juice and finely grated zest of 1 lemon
　(see page 185)
1 tablespoon vanilla extract (essence)
½ teaspoon almond extract (essence)
2 cups (10 oz/315 g) toasted hazelnuts
　(filberts), coarsely chopped (see
　page 185)

*P*reheat an oven to 325°F (165°C).
🌳 In a bowl, stir together the flour, baking powder, salt and cinnamon. Set aside. In another bowl, combine the butter and sugar. Using an electric mixer set on medium speed, beat the mixture until light and fluffy. Add the eggs, one at a time, beating well after each addition. Beat in the lemon juice and zest and vanilla and almond extracts. Reduce the speed to low and beat in the flour mixture, one third at a time. Fold in the nuts. The dough will be slightly granular.

🌳 Turn the dough out onto a floured work surface and divide it in half. Using the palms of your hands, roll each half into an oval log about 1½ inches (4 cm) in diameter. Place well spaced on an ungreased baking sheet.

🌳 Bake until golden brown, about 30 minutes. Remove from the oven and let rest until cool to the touch. Reduce the oven temperature to 250°F (120°C).

🌳 Cut each log on the diagonal into slices ⅓ inch (1 cm) thick. The slices will flatten slightly when you cut them. Arrange the slices, cut side down, on the ungreased baking sheet and return to the oven. Bake until lightly toasted and the edges are golden brown, about 10 minutes. Let cool either on the pan or on a wire rack.

Biscotti are twice-baked cookies: the dough is shaped into a log, baked and then sliced and baked again to produce a delightfully crunchy texture.

Macedonia di Frutta;
Hazelnut Biscotti

Entertaining Basics

AT ITS SIMPLEST, casual entertaining involves nothing more than cooking food and setting a table as you would for any everyday meal. And there will, most likely, be times when your schedule allows you to do nothing more than that. But with a minimum of extra effort, you can elevate an informal gathering far above the ordinary. In planning the menu, for example, you might wish to consider preparing a homemade pasta, condiment or sauce such as those found among the basic recipes on pages 181–84. Giving a few moments of careful thought to your table settings (pages 186–87), including the simple-but-impressive matter of how to fold your napkins, can go a long way toward making the meal more attractive. Flowers or other decorative arrangements (pages 188–89) and your choice of menu and setting will, in their own way, make the difference between a casual occasion that is pleasantly enjoyable and one that is truly memorable.

Basic Pantry

The fresh pasta, condiments, sauces and other preparations for which recipes are given on the following pages will add an extra dimension to your casual menus. Keep them on hand in your pantry or refrigerator for quick access. Of course, you'll find similar products at good-quality markets and specialty-food stores, and you should feel free to buy them if you are pressed for time. But these staples may also be made at home with relative ease and can be stored easily, ready to help you add a special touch to even the most quickly prepared, informal meals.

Homemade Pasta

MAKES ABOUT 1½ LB (750 G); SERVES 6

Making pasta at home is easy if you have a food processor for mixing the dough and a small hand-cranked pasta machine for rolling it out into thin sheets. The pasta machine can also be used for cutting the dough sheets into a variety of noodles, from narrow tagliarini *to* fettuccine *or* tagliatelle. *Wider noodles, such as* pappardelle, *are easily cut with a pastry wheel. For those who lack a food processor and/or pasta machine, directions for making pasta by hand follow. The pasta dough can be made and the noodles cut up to 8 hours in advance of cooking.*

3 cups (15 oz/470 g) all-purpose
   (plain) flour
1 teaspoon salt
4 eggs
about ½ cup (2½ oz/75 g) cornmeal

*I*n the bowl of a food processor fitted with the metal blade, combine the flour and salt. Break the eggs into a small bowl and whisk together lightly. With the processor motor running, drizzle in the eggs. The ingredients will gather together into a rough mass that will look like cornmeal. Turn off the processor and squeeze a handful of the mixture; it should hold together. Transfer the dough from the processor to a work surface. If the dough is crumbly, add a few drops of water. Now, knead the dough with the palm and heel of your hand, repeatedly pushing it against the surface and turning it, until it is smooth and elastic but not too soft, about 5 minutes.

🌳 Flatten the dough into a disk and place in a plastic bag. Let rest at room temperature for 30–60 minutes.

🌳 Divide the dough into 6 equal portions. Lightly dust 1 portion with flour; keep the remaining portions covered. Set the rollers of a hand-cranked pasta machine at the widest opening. Flatten the portion slightly and crank it through the rollers. Reset the rollers one notch narrower. Lightly dust the dough with flour again, fold it into thirds and pass it through the rollers. Repeat this process, being sure to fold the dough each time and dust it with only enough flour to prevent the dough from sticking. Reduce gradually the width of the rollers, until the dough sheet reaches the desired thinness. When it is very thin, lightly sprinkle a kitchen towel with some of the cornmeal and transfer the pasta to it. Let the pasta dry for about 10 minutes—or less if the air is very dry. It should be neither sticky nor too dry. Repeat with the remaining 5 portions.

🌳 To cut the noodles, using the pasta machine, secure the desired cutting attachment to the machine. Cut the dough sheets into easily manageable lengths and crank each length through the cutter to make pasta strands about ⅜ inch (1 cm) wide for *fettuccine* or *tagliatelle* and a scant ⅛ inch (3 mm) wide for *taglierini*. For *pappardelle*, lay the dough sheet on a floured work surface and, using a pastry wheel, cut into long ribbons about 1 inch (2.5 cm) wide. Transfer the pasta to a large tray and toss with some of the cornmeal to prevent the strands from sticking together. Repeat with the remaining dough sheets, then cover the tray with plastic wrap and refrigerate for up to 8 hours. Remove the noodles from the refrigerator just before cooking.

Hand Method: To make the pasta by hand, mix together the flour and salt on a work surface and shape into a mound. Make a well in the center and add the eggs to it. Using a fork, lightly beat the eggs, and then gradually combine the flour and the eggs. Knead the dough until smooth and elastic but not too soft, about 5 minutes. Let rest as directed, then divide in half and roll out each half on a lightly floured surface as thinly as possible. Let the pasta dry for about 10 minutes, less if the air is very dry. Using a pastry wheel, cut into long strips of desired width.

Fruit Salsa

MAKES ABOUT 1 CUP (8 FL OZ/250 ML)

This spicy-hot tropical fruit salsa can be used in place of the peanut dipping sauce for the satay on page 53. It can also be served with the pork tenderloin (recipe on page 132) in place of the apricot mustard or with grilled fish or roast chicken or turkey. The salsa can be made 4–6 hours before serving.

1 cup (6 oz/185 g) diced mango (see page 184), papaya or pineapple

1 or 2 small fresh chili peppers, seeded, if desired, and minced

1 clove garlic, minced

2 tablespoons sugar

¼ cup (2 fl oz/60 ml) fresh lemon or lime juice

1 tablespoon Thai fish sauce *(nam pla)* or 1 teaspoon anchovy paste, optional

*I*n a bowl, combine the mango, papaya or pineapple, chilies, garlic, sugar, lemon or lime juice and the fish sauce or anchovy paste, if using. Stir to mix well. Cover and refrigerate until serving.

Sun-Dried Tomato Spread

MAKES ABOUT 1½ CUPS (12 FL OZ/ 375 ML)

Serve with cooked vegetables, pasta, grilled fish or spread on pizza or bread. This purée can be made ahead and stored in a covered container in the refrigerator for up to 1 week.

1 cup (8 oz/250 g) chopped, drained oil-packed sun-dried tomatoes (oil reserved)

1 tablespoon minced garlic

4 tablespoons fresh basil leaves, optional

4–6 tablespoons coarsely chopped roasted red bell pepper (capsicum), about 1 medium pepper (see page 185), or 1 medium roasted pepper from a jar, rinsed, drained and coarsely chopped

pinch of cayenne pepper, optional

extra-virgin olive oil

*I*n a food processor fitted with the metal blade or in a blender, combine the tomatoes, garlic, basil, if using, roasted red bell pepper and cayenne pepper, if using. Measure the reserved oil from the tomatoes. Add enough extra-virgin olive oil to measure ¼ cup (2 fl oz/60 ml). Add to the food processor or blender and purée until smooth. Transfer to a covered container and store in the refrigerator.

Tapenade

MAKES ABOUT 1½ CUPS (12 FL OZ/375 ML)

This Provençal olive purée is great on pizza or grilled bread or mashed with hard-cooked eggs for a spread. It is also delicious stuffed under the skin of a roasting chicken, or slathered on grilled fish or tossed with steaming hot pasta. Niçoise olives are small, black, brine-cured olives packed in olive oil. They are available in well-stocked markets and specialty-food stores. Tapenade will keep in the refrigerator for up to 2 weeks.

1 cup (5 oz/155 g) pitted niçoise olives

2 tablespoons capers, rinsed and drained

1 tablespoon minced garlic

2 teaspoons chopped, drained anchovy fillet

½ teaspoon freshly ground pepper

6 tablespoons (3 fl oz/90 ml) extra-virgin olive oil

finely grated zest of 1 lemon or orange, optional (see page 185)

2 tablespoons Cognac, optional

*I*n a food processor fitted with the metal blade or in a blender, combine the olives, capers, garlic, anchovy, pepper, olive oil and the lemon or orange zest and Cognac, if using. Purée until smooth. Transfer to a covered container and store in the refrigerator.

Turkey Stock

MAKES 2–2½ QT (2–2.5 L)

Here is a flavorful turkey stock, made from the carcass of the holiday bird, that can be used for making soups, sauces and rice dishes including the turkey risotto on page 87. This recipe can also be used for making chicken stock, substituting 2 pounds (1 kg) chicken parts for the turkey.

1 turkey carcass, broken up
water, as needed
3 fresh flat-leaf Italian parsley sprigs
2 fresh thyme sprigs
1 bay leaf
1 large yellow onion, coarsely chopped
1 or 2 carrots, peeled and chopped
1 celery stalk, chopped

To make the stock, in a large stockpot, combine the turkey carcass and water as needed to cover the carcass fully. Bring to a boil, regularly skimming off any foam and scum that forms on the surface. Cover, reduce the heat to medium-low and simmer for about 1 hour.

❧ Make a bouquet garni by combining the parsley and thyme sprigs and bay leaf on a small piece of cheesecloth (muslin) and then bringing the corners together and tying securely with kitchen string to form a small bag. When the carcass has simmered for 1 hour, add the bouquet garni, onion, carrots and celery, cover partially and continue to simmer for 1½ hours longer.

❧ Strain the stock through a fine-mesh sieve into a jar or other container and place, uncovered, in the refrigerator. When cooled completely, skim off all the fat that has solidified on top. You should have 2–2½ qt (2–2.5 l) stock. At this point the stock can be covered and refrigerated for up to 2 days.

Pesto

MAKES ABOUT 3 CUPS (24 FL OZ/ 750ML)

Pesto keeps well in the refrigerator for up to 1 week. Be sure to pour a thin layer of olive oil on top; this keeps it from discoloring. It can also be frozen for up to 6 months, but do not add the cheese until after it is defrosted. Use pesto on pasta, pizza, crostini and grilled vegetables. It can also be thinned with olive oil or vinegar for a tasty salad dressing or sauce for grilled fish.

2 cups (2 oz/60 g) firmly packed fresh basil leaves
2 teaspoons minced garlic
2–3 tablespoons pine nuts or walnuts
½–1 teaspoon salt, or to taste
½ teaspoon freshly ground pepper
1 cup (8 fl oz/250 ml) mild olive oil
½ cup (2 oz/60 ml) freshly grated Parmesan cheese

In a food processor fitted with the metal blade or in a blender, combine the basil, garlic, nuts, salt and pepper. (Be cautious when adding the salt, as the cheese that is added later can be quite salty.) Process until well combined. Add ½ cup (4 fl oz/125 ml) of the olive oil and purée using short off-on pulses. Stir between the pulses to blend well. Add the remaining ½ cup (4 fl oz/125 ml) oil and the cheese and process to form a thick purée. Do not overprocess; you want the mixture to have a little texture.

❧ Taste and adjust the salt and pepper. Transfer to a covered container and store in the refrigerator.

Tomato Purée

MAKES ABOUT 6 CUPS (48 FL OZ/1.5 L)

This easy-to-make purée is a good base for pizza toppings or can be used almost any time a simple tomato sauce is needed. If flavorful fresh plum (Roma) tomatoes are in the market, they can be used in place of the canned: Peel and seed 2½ pounds (1.25 kg) fresh tomatoes, coarsely chop them and then simmer until soft. Proceed with the recipe as directed.

1 can (2½ lb/1.25 kg) plum (Roma) tomatoes, seeded and diced
2 tablespoons olive oil
3 tablespoons minced garlic
2 tablespoons dried oregano
salt and freshly ground pepper

In a food processor fitted with the metal blade or in a blender, place the tomatoes and pulse until puréed. Transfer to an enamel or stainless steel saucepan and place over medium heat. Bring to a simmer, then reduce the heat to low and simmer very gently, uncovered, until thick, about 20 minutes.

❧ Stir in the olive oil, garlic and oregano. Season to taste with salt and pepper and additional garlic and oregano, if desired.

Mango Chutney

MAKES ABOUT 4 PINTS (64 FL OZ/2 L)

This chutney can be made 6 months in advance and processed as for Canning Preserves (right). Or it can be made 2–3 weeks ahead and refrigerated. It must stand for at least 1 week before serving, to allow the flavors to mellow.

1 large yellow onion, diced
2 cloves garlic
2 limes, cut into small pieces
¼ lb (125 g) fresh ginger, peeled and thinly
   sliced across the grain
2 cups (16 fl oz/500 ml) cider vinegar
3–4 lb (1.5–2 kg) medium-ripe mangoes,
   peeled, pitted and cut into large dice
   (see right)
2 cups (14 oz/440 g) firmly packed
   brown sugar
1 teaspoon salt
1½ teaspoons ground cinnamon
½ teaspoon ground allspice
½ teaspoon ground cloves
¼ teaspoon cayenne pepper, or to taste
1 cup (6 oz/185 g) raisins

In a food processor fitted with the metal blade or in a blender, combine the onion, garlic, limes and ginger and process until finely chopped. Add 1 cup (8 fl oz/250 ml) of the vinegar and purée until smooth.

Place the mangoes in a large, heavy enameled or stainless-steel pan. Add the onion mixture, brown sugar, salt, cinnamon, allspice, cloves, cayenne and the remaining 1 cup (8 fl oz/250 ml) vinegar. Stir well to combine, then bring to a boil over high heat. Reduce the heat to medium and simmer uncovered, stirring from time to time, until thick, from 45 minutes to 1½ hours. Timing will depend on the thickness and size of the pan. Add the raisins during the last 15 minutes of cooking and stir often from this point on to prevent scorching. The chutney is ready when a

teaspoonful sets up within 2 minutes of being dropped into a frozen saucer or when a candy thermometer registers 215°F (102°C) (see Canning Preserves, right).

Ladle the hot preserves into 4 hot, sterilized pint (16-fl oz/500-ml) canning jars, leaving about ½ inch (12 mm) head space. Top with lids and screw on metal bands. Process in a hot-water bath for 10 minutes. Check for a good seal, then store in a cool, dark place for up to 6 months; refrigerate once opened. Alternatively, pack into covered containers and store in the refrigerator for up to 3 weeks.

Hot Fudge Sauce

MAKES ABOUT 1½ CUPS (12 FL OZ/375 ML)

The fudge sauce can be made up to 2 weeks in advance and stored in the refrigerator.

3 oz (90 g) unsweetened chocolate
1 cup (8 fl oz/250 ml) heavy (double)
   cream
1 tablespoon corn syrup
1 cup (8 oz/250 g) sugar
2 teaspoons vanilla extract (essence)
pinch of salt

In a heavy-bottomed saucepan over medium heat, combine the chocolate, cream, corn syrup and sugar. Cook, whisking often, until the sauce registers 234°–240°F (112°–116°C) on a candy thermometer, the soft-ball stage. To test without a thermometer, scoop out a small amount on a wooden spoon, dip the spoon into ice water and then gather the chocolate mixture between your fingertips; it should feel soft and pliable.

Remove from the heat and stir in the vanilla and salt. Serve immediately or let cool, cover and refrigerate. To reheat, place the sauce in the top pan of a double boiler over simmering water or place in a small saucepan over low heat. Stir until hot.

Dicing a Mango

A mango can be difficult to prepare because the pulpy flesh clings to the pit. One simple method is to cut the flesh away from the pit and then peel the skin off in either of the following two ways.

First, put the mango horizontally on a cutting board and slice lengthwise slightly off-center, cutting off all the flesh from one side of the pit in a single piece. Repeat on the other side of the pit. You should have two large slices and a third section that contains the pit and, around the edge, a thin layer of flesh.

Discard or eat the flesh off the middle section with the pit.

One at a time, hold each section, flesh side up. With the tip of a sharp knife, score the flesh lengthwise and crosswise in a lattice pattern, taking care not to cut through the peel.

Press against the center of the peel to invert, popping out the scored cubes of flesh. Slice the cubes from the peel and use as directed.

Alternatively, slice the mango into off-center sections, as directed above, avoiding the pit. Peel the skin off the two half sections with a sharp knife. Dice or slice as directed in recipe.

Basic Techniques

Canning Preserves

Preserves can be stored for long periods if they are packed into hot, sterilized jars and then processed in a hot-water bath to prevent spoilage. Books on preserving offer charts with specific times and procedures to preserve different kinds of ingredients. The basic steps follow:

❧ Thoroughly wash all jars, metal lids and screw bands. Place them in a large pan, add hot water to cover generously and bring to a full boil. Boil 10 minutes, then remove from the heat and let the jars stand in the water.

❧ Using tongs, drain the jars and, while they are still hot, fill them with the preserves, leaving about ½ inch (12 mm) of head space. Gently tap and shake the jars to force out any air bubbles. Using a dampened cloth, wipe any spillage from the jar mouths, then seal the jars with the lids.

❧ Meanwhile, in a large pot half-filled with water, insert a jar rack or place a folded cloth on the bottom and bring the water to a bare simmer; bring a separate pot of water to a boil. Put the filled jars on the rack or on the cloth and add more boiling water to cover them by at least 1 inch (2.5 cm). Bring the water to a full boil, cover and begin counting processing time; chutneys, jams, marmalades and conserves usually take 10 minutes.

❧ Turn off the heat and remove the jars with canning tongs. After several hours, all of the jars should be sealed. Check the lids by touching them to see if they are concave, indicating a secure seal. If a lid is not concave, refrigerate the preserves and eat within a few weeks.

Toasting and Chopping Nuts

To toast nuts, preheat an oven to 325°F (165°C). Spread the nuts in a single layer on a baking sheet with sides and toast in the oven until they just begin to change color, 5–10 minutes.

❧ Remove from the oven and let cool to room temperature. Toasting loosens the skins of hazelnuts (filberts) and walnuts, which can be removed by wrapping the still-warm nuts in a towel and rubbing against them with your palms.

❧ To chop nuts, spread them on a nonslip cutting surface. Using a chef's knife, carefully chop the nuts with a gentle rocking motion. Alternatively, put a handful or two of nuts in a food processor fitted with the metal blade and use a few rapid on-off pulses to chop the nuts to desired consistency; repeat in batches. Don't process too long or they will turn to paste.

Removing Citrus Zest

The zest is the thin, brightly colored outermost layer of the peel of a citrus fruit. Zest can be removed in a number of ways: Using a zester or a small fine shredder, draw its sharp-edged holes across the fruit's peel to remove the zest in thin strips. Or hold the edge of a paring knife or a vegetable peeler away from you and almost parallel to the fruit's peel and carefully cut off the zest in thin strips, taking care not to remove any of the white pith with it. Use as directed.

❧ For grated zest, rub the fruit's peel over the fine holes of a hand-held grater.

Roasting Peppers

Bell peppers (capsicums) and chili peppers can be roasted by a number of methods. Spear each pepper individually on a long fork and hold it directly over an open flame, turning until the skin is evenly blackened and blistered. Or place the whole peppers on a baking sheet and roast them in a 400°F (200°C) oven or under a broiler (griller), turning occasionally with tongs, until the skins are evenly blackened and blistered.

❧ After roasting, place the charred peppers in a closed paper bag or plastic container until cool enough to handle, about 10 minutes. Then, using your fingers or a knife, peel off the charred skins. Cut the peppers in half and pull out and discard the stems, seeds and ribs. Use the peppers as directed.

Preparing Fresh Ginger

Fresh ginger is available in many food stores and vegetable markets. To prepare fresh ginger, peel away the brown, papery skin from the amount being used. Slice or chop the ginger with a small paring knife or a chef's knife, or grate against the fine holes of a hand-held grater. A Japanese-style porcelain ginger grater, with teeth set about ¼ inch (6 mm) apart, produces a finely grated ginger.

Table Setting & Napkin Folding

No matter how casual the occasion, every conscientious host or hostess wants to make a good impression. The simplest way to do so is with your table setting. From your everyday tableware, select cutlery, dishes, glasses and napkins that not only complement one another but also the colors, shapes and styles of the food being served. For most occasions, you'll prefer to fold the napkins into neat triangles and rectangles, placing them beneath the forks as shown below. For a special effect, try one of the napkin-folding techniques demonstrated at right. The photographs show 20-inch (50-cm) square napkins.

A casual place setting is assembled with everyday tableware that, although informal, is nonetheless appealing, including cutlery, a dinner plate with a checkered rim, a plaid cotton napkin, and glasses for wine and water. Cutlery is arranged in order of use, with the first-course (salad) fork and the dinner fork placed left to right at the plate's left. The dinner knife is set to the right of the plate with the blade facing in; the spoon is at the knife's right. Glasses are in easy reach but clear of the plate and cutlery. Other items, such as a soup plate or a Champagne flute, might be added.

Bouquet

Two napkins of complementary or contrasting colors and patterns may be folded together to create a bouquetlike arrangement. Widely available wooden napkin rings neatly hold the bouquets, which are placed to the left of or on the dinner plate.

1. Open one napkin flat. Place the other napkin on top and rotate 45 degrees, forming an eight-pointed star.

2. Using your fingertips, grasp the centers of the two napkins together and pick them up.

3. Arrange the sides and points of the two napkins into neat overlapping folds. Insert the stem of the resulting bouquet into a napkin ring and pull halfway through. Rearrange the points to form a full, attractive bouquet.

Pointed Pocket

Folded into a tidy pocket, a napkin doubles as a creative holder for a set of flatware, an especially convenient bundle for guests to pick up at a buffet table.

1. Open the napkin flat. Fold it into quarters, rotating it so the open points are at the top.

2. Fold the point of the topmost layer downward until it almost—but not quite—touches the bottom corner.

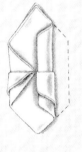

3. Turn the napkin over. Fold the two side corners inward so they meet in the center.

4. Again, fold the sides inward so they meet in the center.

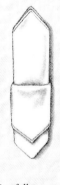

5. Carefully turn the napkin back over to reveal the pocket and tuck cutlery into it. If you like, lightly tie a piece of raffia or ribbon around the napkin just below the pocket.

Nest

Folded into a nest, a napkin becomes a holder for a soup or sauce bowl. The napkin is folded into a progressively smaller square, but, for clarity, illustrations are drawn to the same scale.

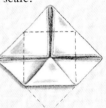

1. Open the napkin flat. Fold each corner inward to meet at the center, to make a smaller square.

2. Again, fold the corners of the napkin inward to meet at the center.

3. Repeat step 2, then carefully turn the folded napkin over. You will have a thick square.

4. Fold the corners of the turned-over napkin toward the center.

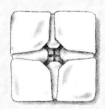

5. Secure the center firmly with your fingertips or with tape, and turn the napkin over again.

6. Holding the center with your finger, peel the layers of corners back with a gentle tugging motion.

187

Flower Arranging

In most cases, floral decorations for a casual occasion will consist of a small bouquet or two of seasonal flowers simply arranged in a vase or other suitable container. They should be displayed in a way that shows them off at their best without calling undue attention or blocking guests' view of one another across the table. Occasionally, however, you might wish to put together a more unique centerpiece, or a decoration for a side table or mantel, that underscores the significance of a particular party. The three arrangements shown here add just such an interesting touch, while maintaining an essentially informal tone.

1. Cut fabric as long as twice the circumference of the pot's rim and 12 inches (30 cm) wide. Place wrong side up, fold both sides to the center and secure the seam with masking tape.

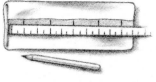

2. With a ruler and pencil, mark the tape in the middle and 2 inches (5 cm) from each end. Then mark the remaining length at regular intervals of 2–3 inches (5–7.5 cm).

3. For every mark on the tape, cut one 6-inch (15-cm) length of florist's wire.

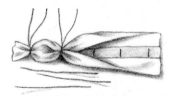

4. Starting at one end, gather the fabric together at each mark, concealing the tape inside. Lightly twist a piece of wire around each gather to secure it in place.

Swagged Flowerpot

Small potted plants already growing in your home—or purchased from a local nursery or florist—easily become attractive living decorations. A view of their soil, however, can be unpleasant in close proximity to food, so it is best to conceal the base of the plant. Sphagnum moss, available where plants are sold, offers one attractive, natural solution. Or with some inexpensive fabric scraps, tape and florist's wire, you can fashion swags that transform each pot into a colorful, country-style decoration, (see pages 104–105).

5. Starting at one end of the swag, secure the ends of a wire twist inside the pot's rim with masking tape. Continue tucking the swag around the pot and securing the wires inside. Place the plant inside the swagged pot.

Vegetable Potager

In spring or summer, fresh herbs and baby vegetables make visually appealing decorations—and serve as a healthy treat to be nibbled on by your guests. Any assortment of small containers in sizes and shapes that are easily grouped together can display them. Or, as shown here, create an attractive centerpiece using small terra-cotta pots stacked to construct a grouping that recalls, in miniature, the provender of a French country garden, or *potager*, (see pages 176-77).

1. Using glue, attach sheet moss or carpet moss to cover the top and edges of a piece of circular particle board or an upturned old circular tray.

2. Stack 2 good-sized terra-cotta pots and glue or place them securely in the center of the moss.

3. Arrange and secure smaller pots of varying sizes and heights around the center pots, to form a pleasing composition. Plant pots with fresh herb plants and baby vegetables.

Flowers, Fruit and Foliage

Arranged in a container scaled to the setting, flowers, small fruit and foliage may be combined to form a unique, natural centerpiece. The tall arrangement shown here would be most suitable for a mantel or sideboard; lower, more horizontal versions could serve as casual table centerpieces. Here, garden roses, tulips and freesias are combined with kumquats wired onto several pear branches using the technique pictured below.

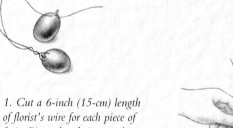

1. Cut a 6-inch (15-cm) length of florist's wire for each piece of fruit. Pierce the fruit near the stem end with the wire. Twist the wire together making a knot close to the stem.

2. Attach each piece of fruit to a branch close to a cluster of leaves or to a small notch in the branch. Twist the wire around the branch to secure the fruit and camouflage the wire. Tie on as many pieces of fruit as you want.

3. Cut Oasis (florist's foam) to fit snugly inside your container. Submerge the foam in water for a full 5 minutes, then place the foam in your chosen container. Using a sharp knife, carefully peel the bark off the bottom 2–3 inches (5–7.5 cm) of each branch and hammer ends until broken to absorb water. Insert branches into the foam.

4. Form a well-balanced, natural-looking composition by filling in the gaps between branches with small groups of seasonal cut flowers.

189

INDEX

CREDITS

Unless otherwise noted, all items pictured are from private collections.

INTRODUCTION
Page 9: "Nantucket" teapot and sugar bowl, "Strawberry and Vine" teacups and pitcher — Waterford Wedgwood.

WELCOME HOME DINNER
Pages 12–13: Candles — Pottery Barn. **Pages 14–15:** Flowers — Silver Terrace Nurseries. Green charger — Sue Fisher King. Grape leaf napkin — Fillamento. **Pages 20–21:** Serving spoon — Sue Fisher King.

AFTER-WORK SUPPER
Pages 24–25: Wine glasses —Fillamento. **Page 26:** Martini glass, square silver bowl — Sue Fisher King. **Page 27:** Napkin, Bridgewater salad plate — Candelier. Maryse boxer bowl — Fillamento. Place mat — Forrest Jones. **Page 30:** Napkin — Sue Fisher King. **Page 31:** Lemon reamer — Williams-Sonoma. **Pages 34–35:** Glass bowl, compotes — Fillamento. Napkin — Williams-Sonoma. Metal "Bongo" vase — Pottery Barn.

AUTUMN SUNDAY SUPPER
Pages 36–37: Basket — Rod McLellen Company. Iron candleholder — Pottery Barn. **Page 38:** Teapot, clay teacups — Fillamento. **Pages 38–39:** Napkin ring, black stoneware plate, glasses — Fillamento. Bamboo-handled flatware — Sue Fisher King. **Page 41:** Orchids — Rod McLellan Company. Red laquer chair — T. Keller Donovan. **Page 44:** Dot soup bowl — Fillamento.

DATE DINNER FOR TWO
Pages 46–47: Tin vase — Fioridella. Dot glass, linen napkins — Fillamento. Gold-edged tumblers, napkin rings — The Gardener. Dinner plates, votives — Sue Fisher King. **Pages 48–49:** Pewter vase — Sue Fisher King. Tin vase — Fillamento. **Page 49:** Amber glass plate — The Gardener. Flatware — Pottery Barn. **Page 55:** Napkin, square bowl — Fillamento. Oval glass dish — The Gardener. **Page 56:** Cream demitasse cups, mother-of-pearl–handled spoons — Sue Fisher King. **Pages 56–57:** Wood chargers, black-edged plates, napkins — Fillamento.

DINNER WITH DEAR FRIENDS
Pages 58–59: Raffia table runner — Bell'occhio. Plants — Silver Terrace Nurseries. Chairs — Pottery Barn. Flatware, celadon plates, soup pot — Forrest Jones. Trunks, sailboat, glove, binoculars — Beaver Bros. Antiques. Palm tree print — Candelier. **Page 60:** Green batik napkin — Sue Fisher King. Woven place mat, glasses — Forrest Jones. Tray, glass decanter, ice bucket, corkscrew, glass pitcher — Beaver Bros. Antiques. **Page 61:** Iron lantern — Candelier. **Page 66:** Palm tree plates — Sue Fisher King. Wooden salad bowl and servers — Forrest Jones.

TREE-TRIMMING SUPPER
Pages 68–69: Cashmere throw, suede pillows, taffeta sachets — Sue Fisher King. Fireplace garland — Laura Lorenz. Douglas Fir tree — Marnie Donaldson. Ribbon — Paulette Knight. **Page 70:**

Toile cachepots — Sue Fisher King. Topiaries, greens, wreath — Laura Lorenz. **Page 71:** Flatware — Sue Fisher King. Utensil caddy — Pottery Barn. Goblets and plates — RH. Cream plates — Candelier. **Page 72 (inset):** Twig tray — RH. Patterned bowl — Sue Fisher King. **Page 73:** Yellow quilted tablecloth, green "woven" bowl — Sue Fisher King. Cheese grater — Forrest Jones. **Page 75:** Pedestal salad bowl, silver-handled salad servers — Fillamento. Green glass plates — RH. Yellow print napkin —Vanderbilt & Company. **Page 76:** Lavender bushels — Pottery Barn. **Page 77:** Glass ramekins — Forrest Jones. Cordial glasses — Fillamento. Wood-handled teaspoons — Sue Fisher King. Candles — Pottery Barn.

AFTER THE HOLIDAYS
Page 81: Metal flatware — Pottery Barn. Yellow-rimmed plates — RH. **Pages 82–83:** Dish towel and napkin — Williams-Sonoma. Bowls — Biordi Imports. **Page 84:** Pottery platters — Biordi Imports. Metal serving pieces — Pottery Barn. **Pages 86–87:** Copper-colored plates — RH. **Pages 88–89:** Cup and saucer — RH. Metal teaspoons — Pottery Barn.

SOUP SUPPER BY THE FIRE
Pages 90–91: Coconut boxes, ebony flatware — Sue Fisher King. Metal urns and fruit candelabra — Brambles. Napkins — RH. **Page 91 (inset):** Leaf votive holder — Brambles. Beeswax candle — Pottery Barn. **Page 92:** Glazed pots — Sue Fisher King. Wine glasses — Fillamento. **Page 93:** Striped plate — Fillamento. Napkin — RH. **Pages 94–95:** Soup tureen with lid — RH. Dishware, salt and pepper grinders — Fillamento. **Pages 96–97:** Striped salad bowl, black salad plates — Fillamento. **Page 97:** "Leaf" plate — RH.

KITCHEN BREAKFAST
Pages 104–105: Potted flowers — Silver Terrace Nurseries. Embroidered napkin, shell-patterned flatware — Williams-Sonoma. Luneville pottery — Forrest Jones. Red place mats — Fillamento. Stools — Pottery Barn. Fabric on flowerpots — Pierre Deux. **Page 105 (inset):** Tea strainer, teapot, trivet, striped cup and saucers, teapot infuser — Williams-Sonoma. **Pages 106–107:** Tumblers, goblets, glass pitcher — Williams-Sonoma. **Page 112:** French-press coffee pot — Forrest Jones. Coffee grinder and canister — Williams-Sonoma.

FAMILY BIRTHDAY PARTY
Pages 114–115: Napkins, glasses — RH. Glazed vases, footed compotes — Fillamento. Mutli-colored plates — Sue Fisher King. Woven napkin rings, "Montana" flatware — Pottery Barn. Flowers — Silver Terrace Nurseries. **Page 115 (inset):** Blue frosted vase — Pottery Barn. **Pages 116–117:** Basket — Forrest Jones. Gift cards, plate — Sue Fisher King. **Page 118 (inset):** Glass decanters — Fioridella. **Pages 118–119:** Glass bowls, wire tray — RH. **Pages 120–121:** Platter — Virginia Brier. Souffle dish in basket — Forrest Jones. Checked bowl — Tancredi & Morgan. **Page 123:** Aqua bowl—Fillamento. Yellow plates — RH. **Pages 124–125:** Striped plate, tablecloth — Sue Fisher King. Green bowl — Pottery Barn. Blue napkins — RH

BACKYARD BARBECUE
Pages 126–127: Chairs, table, straw hats, candleholders — Gardeners Eden. Yellow bowl — Sue Fisher King. Baskets — Chambers/Gardeners Eden. Tumblers, wicker carafes — Pottery Barn. Dish towels and potholder — Williams-Sonoma. **Page 127:** Chair — Pottery Barn. Green pot — Gardeners Eden. **Page 129:** Metal container — Gordon Bennett. Concrete urns — Gardeners Eden and American Ornament. Antique crock — Judy Goldsmith. **Pages 130–131:** Yellow tray — Pottery Barn. **Page 133:** Red straw hat — Forrest Jones. **Page 134:** Red flatware — Judy Goldsmith. **Page 135:** Serving spoons — Forrest Jones. **Pages 136–137:** Glass oval baker — Forrest Jones.

BRUNCH FOR HOUSEGUESTS
Pages 138-139: Tablecloth — Ralph Lauren Home Collection Fabric. Pillows, frosted-glass and metal pedestals, frosted tumblers, goblets, blue-rimmed pitcher — Pottery Barn. Blue pitcher — Fillamento. **Page 140:** Frosted vases — Pottery Barn. **Page 141:** White charger, frosted-handle flatware — Sue Fisher King. **Page 142:** Frosted bowl and plate, silver servers — Fillamento. **Page 142:** Peppermill, dish towel — Williams-Sonoma. **Page 147:** Moon-and-stars plate, white cups, saucers, mugs —Fillamento.

ENGAGEMENT PARTY
Pages 148–149: Sangría glasses — Williams-Sonoma. **Page 150:** Ribbon — Paulette Knight. Gift cards — Brown Bag. Glass pitcher — Antique Dept., Williams-Sonoma Post Street. **Pages 154–155:** Terra-cotta dish — Forrest Jones. "Casbah" serving pieces — Pottery Barn. Mortar and pestle — Biordi Imports. **Page 157:** Cherry pitter — Williams-Sonoma.

WEEKEND CARD PARTY
Pages 158–159: Striped tablecloth — Laura Ashley Home Fabric. White urn — Candelier. Flowers — Silver Terrace Nurseries. **Page 159 (inset):** "Strawberry and Vine" pitcher — Waterford Wedgwood. **Page 160:** Flowerpot napkin ring — Pottery Barn. **Pages 160-161:** Giotto wineglasses — Sue Fisher King. Napkin — Pottery Barn. **Page 161:** Pencil holder, frame and book — Oggetti. **Page 162:** "Strawberry and Vine" plate — Waterford Wedgwood. **Pages 164–165:** Square ivy plate — Waterford Wedgwood. **Page 168:** Teaspoons — Sue Fisher King. **Page 169:** "Nantucket" teapot and sugar bowl, "Strawberry and Vine" teacups and pitcher — Waterford Wedgwood. Cards, scorepad and pencil — Oggetti.

CASUAL PIZZA PARTY
Pages 170–171: Place mats, napkins — Candelier. Flatware — Williams-Sonoma. Glasses — Pottery Barn. **Page 172:** Basket and aprons — Forrest Jones. **Page 173:** Stemmed glasses, terra-cotta pot — Pottery Barn. **Page 175:** Checked dish towel — Williams-Sonoma. Cordovan bowls — RH. **Page 177:** Antique orchid pots — Gordon Bennett. **Page 178:** Glass-footed bowl — Antique Dept., Williams-Sonoma Post Street. **Page 179:** Large footed bowl — Gordon Bennett. Ceramic bowls — Williams-Sonoma.

SOURCES (USA):

American Ornament, (415) 543-1363
Beaver Bros. Antiques, (415) 863-4344
Bell'occhio, (415) 864-4048
Biordi Italian Imports, (415) 392-8096
Brambles, (707) 433-1094
The Brown Bag, (415) 922-0390
Candelier, (415) 989-8600
Chambers, (800) 334-9790
Fillamento, (415) 931-2224
Fioridella, (415) 775-4065
Forrest Jones Inc., (415) 567-2483
The Gardener, (510) 548-4545
Gardeners Eden, (800) 822-9600
J. Goldsmith Antiques, (415) 771-4055
Gordon Bennett, (415) 929-1172
Laura Lorenz Floral Styling and Events, (510) 652-1746
Oggetti, (415) 346-0631
Pottery Barn, (800) 922-5507
Paulette Knight, (415) 626-6184
Pierre Deux, (415) 296-9940
RH, (415) 346-1460
Rod McLellan Co., (415) 362-1520
Sue Fisher King Co., (415) 922-7276
Silver Terrace, (415) 543-4443
T. Keller Donovan, (212) 759-4450
Tancredi & Morgan, (408) 625-4477
Virginia Brier, (415) 929-7173
Vanderbilt & Co., (707) 963-1010
Waterford Wedgwood, (415) 391-5610
Williams-Sonoma, (800) 541-2233
Williams-Sonoma Post Street store, (415) 362-6904

❧

ACKNOWLEDGMENTS

The publishers would like to thank the following people and organizations for their assistance and support in producing this book. For lending, giving or making props: Chuck Williams; Alexandre Saporetti; Kevin Littlefield of Pierre Deux; Marnie Donaldson; Iris Fuller and her group at Fillamento; Sue Fisher King and her team; Rick Herbert and Chris Moss of RH; Marty, Phillipe and Forrest of Forrest Jones; and Connie, Travis and Mr. and Mrs. Robert Ruggieri of Silver Terrace Nurseries. Thanks also to: D. Scott Ruegg, Mr. and Mrs. Ruegg, Carol Davis and Stephen W. Griswold. For food prep assistance: Daniel Becker and Nette Scott. For photography assistance: Brian Mahany. For styling assistance: Tessa Barroll. For their editorial and design help: Maria Cianci, Ken Dellapenta, and Yolande Bull. For their general advice and location information: Stephanie Le Gras of 20 Ross Commons, Jim Caldwell, Phoebe Ellsworth, Sara Bennett, Sally Tantau of Tantau Designs, Margo Tantau Kearney, Keven Clancy, Sharon Lott, Wade Bentson and Al Karstensen.

The following people kindly provided the use of their homes and properties as settings for the menus in this book: Barbara, Spencer and Lindsay Hoopes; Stephen Shubel; Ivy Rosequist; Beth and John Allen; Kaye and Eric Herbranson; Tom Dunker and Barbara Brooks; William and Kathleen Collins of Collins Vineyards; Richard Crisman and Jeff Brock; John and Kittina Powers; Mr. and Mrs. Stephen W. Griswold; Mary and Howard Lester; Wendely Harvey; and John and Dawn Owen.